POETRY AND CRISIS

POETRY AND CRISIS

BY

MARTIN TURNELL

LONDON

SANDS: THE PALADIN PRESS

15 KING ST., COVENT GARDEN, W.C.2

PRINTED IN GREAT BRITAIN
BY THE WHITEFRIARS PRESS LTD.
LONDON AND TONBRIDGE
FOR SANDS : THE PALADIN PRESS
FROM 15 KING ST., COVENT GARDEN
LONDON, W.C.2

FIRST PUBLISHED 1938

29440

FOR A. R. BIRLEY

CONTENTS

vii

NOTE

IN the essay that follows I have tried to outline the relations between religion and literature and to state the attitude of a Catholic towards the literature of our own time. It is impossible to provide anything like an adequate account in the space of an essay and I merely offer it as a handbook for discussion. If it succeeds in stimulating discussion it will have served its purpose.

Parts of this essay have appeared in the *Colosseum* and *The Catholic Herald*. I am indebted to the editors of those periodicals for permission to reprint them here. The first section of Chapter V was published in the Marxist number of *Arena*.

Acknowledgements are also due to the following authors and publishers for kindly allowing me to quote from copyright works: to Mr. Middleton Murry and Messrs. Jonathan Cape for *To the Unknown God*; to Dr. I. A. Richards and Messrs. Kegan Paul, Trench, Trubner for *Science and Poetry*; to Mr. T. S. Eliot and Messrs. Faber and Faber for *Selected Essays* and *Essays Ancient and Modern*, and to the same publishers for *The Defence of the West*; to the Oxford University Press for *The Letters of Gerard Manley Hopkins* and *Countries of the Mind, II*; to Messrs. Chatto and Windus for *Determinations*; and to Messrs. Charles Scribner's Sons and Messrs. Constable for *Interpretations of Poetry and Religion*.

M. T.

POETRY AND CRISIS

CHAPTER I

THE POSITION OF THE PROBLEM

" We tend to think and feel in terms of the art we like : and if the art we like is bad, then our thinking and feeling will be bad.   And if the thinking and feeling of most of the individuals composing a society is bad, is not that society in danger ?   To sit on committees and discuss the gold standard are doubtless public-spirited actions. But not the only public-spirited actions.   They also serve who only bother their heads about art."   (Aldous Huxley, *Texts and Pretexts*, p. 1.)

WE have all ' bothered our heads ' a good deal over the proper place of art in a philosophy of life, and in many respects our uneasiness is a healthy sign. One of the essentials of the Good Life is a philosophy which is capable of taking the whole of life into account and in which the proper relations between the different human activities are clearly defined. Otherwise, some activities tend inevitably to assume a disproportionate importance, or to become substitutes for one another.

This has happened in the case of art and the results have been serious.   Art has to a large extent replaced religion and metaphysical thinking.   As a corollary to this, there has been an enormous increase in the influence of the written word, particularly in its least salutary forms.   It is no doubt easy to exaggerate the number of people who deliberately go to a particular novelist for their ' philosophy,' but the fact that it is to imaginative writers that the public, whether consciously or not, is more and more inclined to turn, is one that we can hardly overlook. We must of course distinguish. A great writer—the late D. H. Lawrence is a case in point—is the possessor of a certain wisdom which, properly understood, may be of immense value to the reader. But it needs to be carefully sifted and the good separated from the bad (as with Lawrence's views on sex) and tested by eternal principles. What is harmful, is the uncritical acceptance of an artist's wisdom as though it were a complete 'philosophy' without any reference to first principles. It is because the reading public as a whole, as T. S. Eliot lately pointed out,[1] is without any body of principles of this sort that it is to-day at the mercy of an army of writers whose chief effect is to impose on it a secularist outlook.

The purpose of the present essay is to trace the genesis of the modern attitude and to see whether the critic is able to do anything to remedy it.

The problem arises directly out of the conditions in which we live. There may be a tendency among Catholics to treat the middle ages as a golden age and to forget that medieval society was in many respects a primitive one. But primitive or not, the problem in its modern form did not exist for the middle ages any more than it did for ancient Greece. In both periods culture was one. There was a great measure of agreement about the universe, about the external world and about the 'nature and destiny of man'. Society was stable, was based on generally accepted principles. It is true—and it was the weakness of the Schoolmen as well as of Plato—that poetry as distinct from the more useful arts of painting and architecture was often regarded with suspicion, even with hostility. But on the whole it was recognised that all human

---

[1] *Essays Ancient and Modern*, London, 1936.

activities are good and the activity of the artist had its place in the scheme, whether his art was used to build churches or simply to give pleasure to his fellow-men. There was in fact a close relation between art and the life of the people, particularly what is loosely known as ' the spiritual life '. This state is a healthy one. Art has a place of its own in life. It is not a substitute for anything else ; it has no need of apologists. It is simply there.

" When artists set about speculating on their art ", wrote the Père de Munnynck,[1] " it is always a trifle disquieting. Perfectly healthy people are scarcely aware of their internal organs : one is not bothered with one's liver or stomach or kidneys until they begin to ' crock up '."

It is remarkable that in spite of the puritanical attitude of the middle ages towards poetry, it was only with the coming of the European Renaissance and the destruction of the old order that men began to feel the need of justifying and explaining their art. The literary criticism of the Greeks or of pre-Renaissance writers was on the whole of a severely practical kind. Aristotle's *Poetics* is primarily a guide to playwriting ; the effects of drama on the audience, which have engaged students so much, occupy a very small proportion of his treatise. The criticism of a poet like Dante, for example, is concerned neither with the place of poetry in life nor with the nature of inspiration, but with practical matters like versification and language. And the same is true of the earlier English critics like Campion and Daniel.

As civilisation becomes more complex, a certain discussion of the value of poetry to society is natural and healthy—as long as it is related, as modern critics

[1] *Colosseum*, March, 1934, pp. 27-8.

B 2

do not always relate it, to a general body of principles. This sort of concern, however, is very different from the concern of Renaissance critics. Men suddenly became uneasy and perplexed and began to ask : What is art ? What is its function ? " The first task of Renaissance criticism ", wrote Spingarn, [1] " was the justification of imaginative literature." Moral preoccupations begin at once to overshadow practical ones. We find an intellectual of the stamp of Sir Philip Sidney feeling the need of justifying the art he practises on moral grounds and going to absurd lengths, in the *Apologie for Poesy*, to explain away the banishment of poets from Plato's Republic.

Sidney was no isolated example. The question has been asked and answered according to his lights by nearly every responsible critic since his time. The following is a representative selection of answers :

1. " The use of this *feigned history* (*i.e.*, poetry) hath been to give a shadow of satisfaction to the mind of man in those points wherein the nature of things doth deny it." (Bacon.)

2. " A just and lively image of human nature, representing its passions and humours, and the changes of fortune to which it is subject, for the delight and instruction of mankind." (Dryden.)

3. " More and more mankind will discover that we have to turn to poetry to interpret life for us, to console us, to sustain us. Without poetry, our science will appear incomplete ; and most of what now passes with us for religion and philosophy will be replaced by poetry." (Arnold.)

4. " If in the seventeenth century anyone had taken it into his head to ask Molière or Racine why they wrote, they would probably only have been able to answer : To amuse decent people. It was only with the advent of romanticism that literature came to be

---

[1] *Literary Criticism in the Renaissance*, 1899, p. 1.

4

regarded as an attack on the absolute and its result a revelation." (Jacques Rivière.)

5. "The demand which the human soul makes is for satisfaction here and now ; men's eyes must *see* their salvation. It is this visible salvation that great poetry does offer." (Middleton Murry.)

6. "It [poetry] is capable of saving us." (I. A. Richards.)

7. "Art has two great functions. First it provides an emotional experience. And then, if we have the courage of our own feelings, it becomes a mine of practical truth." (D. H. Lawrence.)

Although all these writers agree that poetry is not merely valuable, but very valuable to society, there is little agreement about the exact nature of this value. In modern times, from Arnold to Richards, poetry is valued chiefly as a substitute for something else. It is no longer Dryden's ' delight and instruction of mankind,' but something ' capable of saving us.' In other words, its whole position in the present order has undergone a drastic change. For Arnold, as for Richards, it seems intended to provide an outlet for emotions which were previously associated with institutional religion. Middleton Murry is prepared to go even further : he thinks that the function of poetry is not only to provide us with a knowledge of the world in which we live, but also to *create* the values by which we live—a function hitherto performed by religion.

This side of modern critical theory will be discussed in a later chapter. Meanwhile, the argument can, perhaps, be made clearer by sketching a tentative theory of the value of poetry.

From the foregoing list a number of positive conclusions emerge. Poetry provides us with a valuable *imaginative experience*—an experience, moreover, that is usually denied to people who are not poets (Bacon). According to Dryden it gives pleasure and knowledge. Lawrence proceeds to emphasise the *emotional* nature of the poetic experience, but also suggests that it is in some way connected with ' truth '.

All this is true, but it remains to integrate these fragments into some sort of system. Otherwise we have no means of deciding what is meant by words like ' truth ', ' knowledge ', ' emotion '. In discussing poetry, the first question we have to answer is : What is man ? Unless we know what man *is*, we cannot possibly know what experiences are valuable for him. I am inclined to distrust philosophies which define the world in terms of human need, but once we know what man *is*, we can go on to conclude that he has certain needs to satisfy. Man was created by God and naturally desires God. He is a combination of body and soul. He is distinguished from other animals by the possession of reason. The mind was made to *know* and naturally desires knowledge. It also has the power of reflecting on its own experience. We can therefore say that man has spiritual and intellectual needs to satisfy. We know from experience that he also has what may for the moment be called ' emotional needs ', and that he usually seeks satisfaction for them in art.

History shows that art is a spontaneous activity. Even in the most primitive societies we find man taking a delight in reproducing the world about him, and his attempts, however crude, have always found willing spectators. In fact art satisfies some *natural* need in man. Moreover, great art is always stimulating and revitalising. It is always, in the language of Aristotle, in some sense an increase of *being*. It is natural that we should have become more conscious of our need for this kind of stimulus since the decay

6

of institutional religion, but there could be no greater mistake than to think that we can live—as some people to-day try to live—by art alone. We may conclude that man has both *religious* and *emotional needs*, and that one *activity* can never be a *substitute* for another without doing violence to his nature, without ending in unhappiness and disillusionment.

I have spoken of intellect and emotion as though they were independent of one another, but it is doubtful whether emotion can ever exist in a pure state independently of intellect. The difficulty is to discover the precise relationship between them in the work of art.

It seems to me that Maritain is right in stressing the intellectual nature of art, but it must be remembered that the poetic activity differs radically from the ordinary process of intellectual abstraction. It is the function of intellect to abstract from sense-experience. Intellect gives the universal, the senses the particular. Now it is of the essence of good art to be concrete, and its very concreteness points to the predominance of the affective elements in experience. For in the work of art the usual function of intellect is modified. It organises our sense-perceptions in such a way that new *combinations of feeling* are created.

" The greatest thing of all ", wrote Aristotle, " is to be a master of metaphor. It is the one thing that cannot be learned from others ; and it is also a sign of original genius, since a good metaphor implies the intuitive perception of the similarity in dissimilars."

Thus in the line

> Lilies that fester smell far worse than weeds

two different images—the fragrant lilies and the suppurating wound—are brought into relation in such a

7

way that a fresh feeling is created. The freshness and novelty of the association, which are the product of an intellectual process, produce the shock of pleasure which is the ' æsthetic experience '.

It follows that though the genesis of the work of art is intellectual, the result is an emotional experience. It can, I think, be said that the great strength of the Aristotelian philosophy lies in its recognition of the importance of the emotional life, as the weakness of the Platonic lies in its failure to understand it. The abiding value of the *Poetics* does not consist in its analysis of the catharsis or the study of dramatic form, but in showing that emotional experience is necessary and valuable to man as he is.

It is often argued that poetry is completely independent of the beliefs on which it rests and that the only criterion is the quality of the experience—the freshness of the vision, the order and intensity of the experience. Now this is only partially true. In an article already referred to, the Père de Munnynck suggests that one of the functions of art is to introduce order into the chaos of our emotional life. But if poetry is to be orderly, to be something more than the mere expression of a man's own disorderly feelings, it can only be by reference to another order outside it which we may call ' truth ' or ' reality '. An emotional experience must necessarily imply some sort of judgement of value. The scholastics speak of a *vis æstimativa;* and I think that we must admit that the appreciation of a poet's emotions involves an appreciation of his valuations (which may be highly perverse). Our estimate of a poet must therefore take into consideration his view of ' reality '.

The relation between art and ' reality ', between the poet's experience and the world as it is, is one of the central problems of criticism. It is a problem which at once assumes different proportions when we get away from purely descriptive poetry to poets like Dante or Shakespeare who present us with a world— a world in which a particular ' philosophy ' or ' view of life ' predominates. It is a question that will be discussed in the next chapter. For the moment it is sufficient to point out that while the medieval poet was living in a ready-made world and was provided by the theologian and the philosopher with his subject-matter, the modern poet, having no such advantage, has tended to create a world of his own. Thus the rôle of the poet has undergone a change. As Dante understood it, it was to realise in terms of feeling what was already known to the mind in abstract form. The close of the *Paradiso* is a good instance. The state of beatitude had been described in abstract terms by the theologian, but it was left to the poet to realise it in concrete terms, to translate philosophy into his medium and consequently to make the experience in a sense accessible to the reader. With the destruction of this ready-made world, there arose a number of different, conflicting philosophies. What we shall have eventually to decide is how far a work of art can be valuable when it is based upon inferences about the universe which the reader regards as mistaken ; and it will also have to be decided how far these changes have affected the quality of the poet's work.

CHAPTER II

POETRY AND CRISIS

WE are often warned by historians against the practice of dividing literature into movements and periods, and labelling them as though these divisions were absolute. But this does not alter the fact that European literature does tend to divide into two distinct sections—medieval and modern—though these include sub-divisions and ' periods '. At the Renaissance one world comes *finally* to an end and another begins. The new world and the new poetry possess qualities undreamed of in the pre-Renaissance world, and our first duty is to recognise the fact. We also have to recognise another fact—the fact that it was precisely the disappearance of other qualities, other beliefs, that made modern poetry and the world it presents possible.

Before going on to discuss the poetry of the two periods, there are one or two reservations to be made. The distinguishing characteristics of the two periods appear to be the presence of religion in medieval literature and its absence from modern literature. Now though the Renaissance seems to be the point at which the change took place, human nature did not of course suddenly change at a given moment. The Renaissance was simply the culminating point of changes which had been going on beneath the surface for generations and were suddenly accelerated. We must remember, for instance, that many of the qualities we most admire in medieval poetry—its freshness, its

spontaneity, its faculty for going straight to the object
—were due to the fact that it was the product of a
civilisation which was young in the sense that con-
temporary civilisation is old. There will be a good
deal to say about introspection and self-analysis in
modern literature; but though both have been
encouraged by the break-up of Christendom and the
decline of metaphysics, and all the social and ideo-
logical consequences, it is certain that literature would
naturally have become more introspective and more
analytical as civilisation grew up. The real trouble
with modern literature, with the *Confessions* of Rous-
seau as opposed to those of Augustine, is not that it
is introspective, but that there is no longer anything
to balance the introspection. Maritain went to the
heart of the matter when he remarked that in order to
be healthy, the introspection of a Proust would have
to be balanced by the spirituality of an Augustine.

When we look at history, more particularly the
history of the Christian era, we see at once that it is
not merely a period of time, of steady progress in the
same direction. It is rather a continual fluctuation
between periods of violent upheaval and concentrated
development, and periods of calm and stability. The
primary fact of Western civilisation is Revolution,
which may be defined as *a sudden re-orientation of society
caused by a common realisation of some new aspect of truth.*
Revolution implies destruction, and it almost invari-
ably entails a preliminary destruction of the existing
order or a part of it, as a prelude to the foundation
of a new order. In this sense the Incarnation is THE
REVOLUTION. It involved the destruction of what was
rotten in contemporary society and the completion
and fulfilment of what was good.

It is from the fact of the Incarnation that any consideration of European literature must start. For Christianity developed—developed in Newman's sense —and finally gave Europe a metaphysic and a *Weltanschauung* which are reflected in a greater or lesser degree in all subsequent literature, even in a negative way in the literature of our own time. If Christianity is in one sense 'the destructive element', we must remember that down to the Renaissance it actually provided the poet with his outlook. It added a completely new dimension to existing literature—a whole new realm of experience—besides preserving what was already there. The periods of instability—the age of Augustine, for instance—were followed by periods of stability like the thirteenth century or the seventeenth century in France.

The modern, or post-Renaissance, period has also been dominated by the idea of Revolution. The Renaissance and the Reformation were both in a sense revolutions. Since then there have been scientific revolutions like the Cartesian, the Copernican and the Darwinian revolutions ; and politico-religious revolutions like the French and Russian Revolutions. It is precisely these other revolutions that have provided the modern poet with his outlook. The point is that the modern revolutions, as far as their effects on the spiritual life of Europe are concerned, have tended to be largely destructive. For 'new truth' can only benefit mankind provided that it is incorporated into a living tradition. Revolution is the process of perpetual renewal without which tradition runs dry and degenerates into dogmatism, as we can see from the end of the middle ages ; but without the directive force of tradition, mankind has no means of consolidating his findings and relating them to the totality of human wisdom. The result is that the destructive side of the revolutionary process gains the ascendancy and ends in anarchy or in a still narrower dogmatism. This is, in fact, what has happened. The new doctrines introduced by the modern revolutions instead of leading to a new order have simply attacked the roots of traditional civilisation and produced a *state of crisis*. They have reduced European unity to a welter of conflicting sects.

The development of culture is a dynamic process. Until the Renaissance, the power behind it was religion. The genius of Christianity, considered as a cultural factor, has always consisted in its power of assimilating and transforming the diverse elements furnished by the surrounding world. This process of assimilation and transformation is Tradition. Now tradition can be used in a variety of senses. We speak of the public school tradition or the English tradition, meaning little more than the *continuity* of certain institutions. When I speak of tradition, I mean the European tradition, and the European tradition is the continuity of a way of life that was largely destroyed at the Renaissance. Its continuity as well as its characteristics were the creation of Christianity and as soon as Christendom broke up, the guarantee behind the European tradition was removed. It would be tempting to discuss the nature of the European tradition, but here it is not possible. Questions of this sort must be left in order to deal concretely with the differences between medieval and modern literature in so far as they are the result of religion.

II

I shall begin by setting out the traditional view of poetry, then try to show how it has been modified by circumstances over which the artist has no control. The best description of the ' old ' as opposed to the 'new' poetry occurs in Claudel's *Positions et propositions*.[1]

"The object of poetry," he writes, "is not, as people often make out, dreams, illusions and ideas. It is that holy reality (*sainte réalité*) which was created once for all and in which we ourselves are placed. It is the universe of visible things to which Faith joins that of invisible things. It is everything which sees us and which we ourselves see. All that is the work of God who creates the stuff of the greatest poet and of the humblest bird. And just as the *philosophia perennis* does not invent, as great novelists who had mistaken their vocations like Spinoza and Leibnitz invented, abstract beings which no one had seen before their inventors, but is content with the terms provided by reality . . . so there is a *poesis perennis* which does not invent its themes, but takes what creation offers in the manner of the liturgy."

In short, man was living in a clearly defined universe with a heaven above and a hell beneath. The poet was a member of a community united by a common faith. He had a common subject-matter —the visible world as given in sense-experience and that invisible world defined by faith. It is precisely the certainty not only about the existence, but also about the goodness of the created world, that accounts for one of the principal differences between medieval and modern poetry. The point becomes clear if we compare the following passages from representative medieval and modern poems, the opening of *The Prologue* and the opening of *The Waste Land*.

> Whan that Aprille with his shoures sote
> The droghte of Marche hath perced to the rote,
> And bathed every veyne in swich licour,
> Of which vertu engendred is the flour ;

[1] Pp. 165-6.

14

Whan Zephirus eek with his swete breeth
Inspired hath in every holt and heeth
The tendre croppes, and the yonge sonne
Hath in the Ram his halfe cours y ronne,
And smale fowles maken melodye,
That slepen all the night with open yë,
(So priketh hem nature in hir corages) :
Than longen folk to goon on pilgrimages
(And palmers for to seken straunge strondes)
To ferne halwes, couthe in sondry londes ;
And specially, from every shires end
Of Engelond, to Caunterbury they wende,
The holy blisful martir for to seke,
That hem hath holpen, whan that they were seke.

    *   *   *   *

April is the cruellest month, breeding
Lilacs out of the dead land, mixing
Memory and desire, stirring
Dull roots with spring rain,
Winter kept us warm, covering
Earth in a forgetful snow, feeding
A little life with dried tubers . . .

The first difference is the contrast between Chaucer's spontaneous joy in ' the visible sweating universe,' and the mixture of horror and disgust with which Eliot regards it. In one, harmony and stability : in the other, immense uncertainty and unrest. Chaucer rejoicing in something possessed, Eliot overwhelmed by a sense of something irrevocably lost. This is apparent from the details of the passage. Both writers are describing changes that occur in nature with the coming of spring. It is a time of awakening and for the medieval poet awakening means an *increase of life*, a joyful release from the bondage of winter. April showers are ' sweet ' and their virtue is to break up the winter-bound earth. They bring flowers and the fruits of the earth. For Eliot, on the contrary, April is ' the cruellest month ', precisely because it is the end of winter and the beginning of change from insensibility to awakening. Winter is not, as it was for Chaucer, a time of death but of pleasant numbness and insensibility. It is an awakening from which the poet would gladly escape. All that the earth produces is a few flowers. The roots are ' dull ', unwilling to grow. Chaucer is sensible enough of the effects of spring. Birds sing and cannot sleep. Men are revived by the stimulus of the season, are restless and feel the need to travel to foreign lands or to go on pilgrimages after being shut up all winter. In Eliot the effects of spring are narrowly sexual. It brings memories which stir our sluggish desires, but is essentially an unpleasant, morbid state. Whereas Chaucer's is a poetry of acceptance, Eliot's by comparison is a poetry of refusal and as such represents the modern outlook as Chaucer's represents the medieval. This does not mean of course that Eliot is not a great poet, or that he is in any sense an ' escapist '. He is a great poet and his greatness consists precisely in the unflinching honesty with which he faces a tragic situation. It is this honesty, indeed, which gives his finest work its peculiar strength and toughness.

Perhaps the most striking fact about the two passages is the difference of focus. The medieval poet is interested primarily in *things*—a point to which I shall return—and his poem is a record of reactions to them. The balance of the poem comes from the close correspondence between emotion and the object which evokes it. In the modern poet, the process is reversed. The poem is the analysis of a state of mind and the connection with spring and the use of a vocabulary drawn from spring in a way fortuitous and subjective. In other words, the poet is not describing spring nor even his sensations in spring : he is equating spring awakening with a certain mood, and simply uses terms drawn from spring in order to exteriorise certain

very personal feelings. For instance, I take the
lines :

mixing

> Memory and desire . . .
> Winter kept us warm, covering
> Earth in a forgetful snow . . .

to refer to a state of mind which has been made
impossible (so the poet implies) by the advance of
knowledge and the decline of religious belief, or
what Dr. I. A. Richards calls ' the neutralisation of
nature '. Thus the desire for new life is ' mixed ' with
a wistful memory of a former state of ignorance
described as ' winter '.

The whole point is that for the medieval poet,
whether he was aware of it or not, the goodness of
the natural world consisted in the fact that it was
God-given. The natural presupposed the super-
natural from which it sprang. Now one of the
functions of religion—of the supernatural—is to *con-
serve* the natural world and natural human instincts.
We therefore find that once the supernatural is denied,
as it was, for example, by the French naturalist school
in the nineteenth century, the natural withers and
dwindles into an unnatural, inhuman materialism.
This leads to one of the central problems of criticism.

The disappearance of the common outlook and
the inevitable division of contemporary culture into
a vast number of tiny independent cells, forces the
literary critic into a distinction which looks at first
sight like the old distinction of form and content, but
in reality is nothing of the sort. The critic begins his
study by an examination of the poet's language and
style, but it is a mistake to think, as people are some-
times disposed to think, that his work ends there.
He has to go on to criticise the poet's outlook and his
choice of subject. There is no greater fallacy than to

assume that subject-matter is of no importance, for this is simply to admit that there *is* a difference between form and content. The poet's subject, his outlook, his range of feeling are all functions of his sensibility ; and his sensibility in turn is determined by the condition of culture and the poet's beliefs.

The problem of the place of belief in poetry arises in its acutest form in studying medieval poetry. I think we can say that the value of Dante or Chaucer or Villon, different as these writers are, lies chiefly in the feeling of stability, the belief in a fixed, unchanging order of nature that they succeed in communicating to the reader, whereas the appeal of the modern poet lies precisely in the felt absence of these things, in the sense of tension from which his work springs. The recent controversies over poetry and beliefs started from the assumption that a definite belief on the part of the poet was an obstacle which the reader has to overcome, and that an absence of belief is the most favourable condition for writing poetry. Actually, it seems to me that the reverse of this is the truth. The real issue is not whether the *reader* needs to share the poet's beliefs in order to enjoy his poetry to the full, but whether a belief, a system, enables the *poet* to write better. In his remarkable paper on ' The Absence of Religion in Shakespeare ', Professor George Santayana, who can scarcely be suspected of partiality, comes to the conclusion that it does.

" Shakespeare . . . " he writes, " is remarkable among the greater poets for being without a philosophy and without a religion. In his drama there is no fixed conception of any forces, natural or moral, dominating our mortal energies. . . . Those of us, however, who believe in circumnavigation, and who think that both human reason and human imagination require a certain totality in our views . . . we can hardly find in Shakespeare all that the highest poet could give. Fulness is not necessarily wholeness, and the most profuse wealth of characterisation seems still inadequate, if this picture is not somehow seen from above and reduced to a dramatic unity. . . .

" For what is required for theoretic wholeness is not this or that system but some system. Its value is not the value of truth, but that of victorious imagination. *Unity of conception is an æsthetic merit no less than a logical demand.*" [1]

' Fulness is not wholeness '—this is the most penetrating criticism of post-Renaissance poetry that I know. It is precisely this ' wholeness ' that the medieval poet had to give. When Dante wrote the celebrated line :

e la sua voluntate è nostra pace

he was not making an isolated statement. Still less was he producing the line of ' pure poetry ' for which Arnold seems to have taken it. His line has behind it the *whole* of *The Divine Comedy*—the whole force of a clear, consistent and coherent attitude towards the universe is packed into the line and gives it its tremendous power.

We may not care much for the sort of experience Dante has to offer ; we may perhaps prefer other forms of intensity. But these personal preferences ought not to blind us to the fact that ' wholeness ', which is always the outcome of ' some system ', of some beliefs, is an æsthetic value. Nor should they lead us to assume that *objectively considered* ' wholeness ' is necessarily inferior to ' fulness '.[2]

---

[1] *Interpretations of Poetry and Religion*, London, 1900, pp. 163–4. (Italics mine.)
[2] Professor Santayana's contention that Shakespeare is ' without a philosophy and without a religion ' is, of course, open to criticism in certain respects. I find it difficult to believe in the complete spiritual neutrality which the Professor seems to attribute to him. I

III

At the Renaissance the stability, which pervades almost every line that Dante wrote, was finally destroyed as far as a large section of European society was concerned. The old world comes to an end and the new world begins. It is true that the Renaissance led to discoveries about man, about the outer world ; but the enormous delight of the Renaissance in nature and in man involved a sundering of God and man who had been joined in the Incarnation, of nature and the supernatural as defined above. There is a sense that nature and man are both independent of anything outside them, and consequently a failure to relate experience to unchanging principles which had become perfectly natural to the medieval mind.

It is easy to see how it was that the Renaissance inaugurated a period of doubt. Man was no longer a member of a community united by a common faith. He was independent—an isolated individual with no authority save his own experience. He began to doubt the existence of God and God's interest in his destiny, until finally he came to doubt the existence of the visible world and even his own identity. Now, the great paradox of the Renaissance is that in spite of its worship of the world, it marked the beginning of a movement away from this world—not a spiritual or ascetic movement, but a definite *retreat* inwards. Underlying the traditional world-view was the

think we have to distinguish between a philosophy in the sense that Epicureanism was Lucretius's, or Thomism Dante's philosophy, and a *Weltanschauung* or ' philosophy of life ' in the sense that some of Shakespeare's tragedies are thought to present us with a ' philosophy '. The strength of Lucretius and Dante lies in the fact that their philosophy and their *Weltanschauung* are identical, or to be more exact, that their outlook is the outcome of clearly apprehended principles. For the modern poet, one feels, the *Weltanschauung* exists without any corresponding philosophical system and may actually become a substitute for a system. The outlook behind ancient poetry is on the whole *intellectual* and the outlook behind modern poetry *emotional*.

classical metaphysic with its emphasis on *being* and its confidence in the findings of the *sensus communis*. But this, too, disappears and is replaced by one or other of the idealist systems with their supposed antithesis between *idea* and *reality*. The theory that we can have no conceptual knowledge of the real leads to the conclusion that individual experience is the sole reality. The only thing of which man can be certain is his own experience, and all his speculations begin from the data of consciousness. We get in fact that endless and inordinate speculation about man's mental process which is registered in modern poetry. In other words, we get first a thorough-going subjectivism, and secondly a cult of experience, or more correctly of unrelated sensation, for its own sake which culminates in the work of a diarist like Amiel or a novelist like André Gide.[1]

Middleton Murry insists, in an essay which I shall have to discuss, that Shakespeare is the first 'modern poet'.

" At the beginning of the epoch stands Shakespeare, who comprehends within himself . . . the whole movement of which lesser men were to manifest the phases after him." [2] " We are bound ", he continues, " ever and again and finally to return to Shakespeare in our pursuit of the spiritual history of man since the Renaissance. Up to Shakespeare the spiritual history of man—I speak of the West alone—is comprehended within the Church ; with him it passes outside it." [3]

It is true that Shakespeare's work marks the break-up of Christendom and that in it we detect the sounds

[1] This is interestingly discussed by Professor Saurat in *Modernes*, Paris, 1935, and by Daniel-Rops in *Les Années tournantes*, Paris, 1932.
[2] *To the Unknown God*, p. 182.
[3] *Ibid.*, p. 186.

of tottering beliefs. It is the product of a society which was in the process of losing the faith and itself disintegrating, and the agony involved becomes, in greater or lesser degree, the subject-matter of modern poetry as stability was of medieval poetry. Shakespeare, however, does not belong wholly either to the medieval or the modern worlds. The heart of his poetry is the battle between the medieval mind and Renaissance sophistication. In Shakespeare there appears perhaps for the last time in English poetry the primitive folk-element which, though transformed and raised to the first intensity, was present in all medieval art—in Dante and Chaucer as well as in the carvings at Chartres—*and stamped it as the work of the people as an undivided whole*, as the expression of an experience in which every section of the community had its part. This element appears most clearly in *Henry the Fourth*, Part I, in the contrast between Falstaff and the Bolingbrokes ; but it is also clear that the old social solidarity has gone and that divisions are growing within society. Shakespeare's loathing for ' the multitude ' would have been incomprehensible to Chaucer, who was at once an aristocrat and a man of the people, and so would his concern for the tragic hero.

But Shakespeare is too great to serve as an example for a purpose like our own, and it is to another poet, to John Donne, who also in a sense " comprehends within himself . . . the whole movement of which lesser men were to manifest the phases after him ", that we must turn. Why Shakespeare will *not* and why Donne will serve as an instance is excellently put by T. S. Eliot.

" Donne, Corbière, Laforgue ", he writes,[1] " begin

[1] *A Garland for John Donne*, Cambridge, Harvard University Press, 1931, pp. 15–16.

with their own feelings, and their limitation is that they do not always get much outside or beyond; Shakespeare, one feels, arrives at an objective world by a process from himself, whoever he was, as the centre and starting point. . . . With Donne and the French poets the pattern is given by what goes on in the mind rather than by the exterior events which provoke the mental activity and play of thought and feeling."

Donne is a modern poet because we hear in his verse that instability, that anxiety and unrest which are peculiarly modern. A writer in *Determinations* [1] puts the matter in a nutshell when he remarks:

" Dante, Lucretius and Chapman are disciples rather than metaphysicians themselves; that is, they make no independent approach to reality, but only through another man's work. . . . Dante (he is comparing the *Paradiso* and *The First Anniversary*) presents us with the *fait accompli;* he and Beatrice are at the end of their mystic journey, and it does not trouble him now. Donne, on the other hand, tries to follow Elizabeth Drury point by point : the problem of how the journey was possible interests him at least as much as the fact that it was made."

It is true that Donne's dialectical subtlety is the outcome of the absence of a philosophy. Donne was a metaphysician trying to come to terms with the new world in which he found himself. He was a Christian —Mr. Eliot's criticism is not altogether fair—but he was a Christian in a very different and less assured sense than Dante or Chaucer. The famous passage on the ' new philosophy ' is a concrete expression of the modern outlook.

[1] James Smith in a paper called ' On Metaphysical Poetry " pp. 41–2, 43–4.

And now the Springs and Sommers which we see,
Like sonnes of women after fiftie bee.
And new Philosophy calls all in doubt,
The Element of fire is quite put out ;
The Sun is lost, and th' earth, and no man's wit
Can well direct him where to looke for it.
And freely men confesse that this world's spent,
When in the Planets, and the Firmament
They seeke so many new ; then see that this
Is crumbled out againe to his Atomies.
'Tis all in peeces, all cohaerence gone ;
All just supply, and all Relation. . . .

What is patent and plain in this passage is that the poet no longer has a ready-made philosophy which he can translate into emotional terms. He is on the contrary trying to find his way himself, and poetry is being called upon to perform a fresh function. It is being used by the poet as a substitute for philosophy, or rather the poet is trying to combine the office of poet and metaphysical thinker. What we must be quite clear about is that the poet is neither a professional philosopher nor a follower embodying the thought of another in verse ; he is actually thinking, speculating as he writes. The emotion is generated in the process of thought in such a way that thought itself can never be pure in the sense in which St. Thomas's thought was pure : intellect is being led by the emotions.

If Donne was one of the most important poets of his century, it was because he was at once the last scholastic and the first of the moderns. In him two worlds meet with a difference. The best of Donne's critics, Eliot and Professor Bredvold, have emphasised his uneasiness and this uneasiness is closely connected with Donne's religion. For Donne lived in an age of transition, of change from the medieval to the modern world. It is a change from a state of spiritual unity to the dualism of the contemporary world. A critic, from whom I have already quoted, speaks of his work as " the battle-ground between the difficulty of belief and the reluctance to doubt ".[1]

This puts the matter extremely well. Donne was one of the first great poets to find himself obliged to choose between conflicting outlooks, for whom in short a choice of outlook was a major issue. There had been differences of opinion in the middle ages, but differences within a single philosophy. From Donne onwards a difference of opinion means a complete difference of outlook.

The sort of perplexity and anguish this produced is apparent from Donne's standpoint in the religious dissensions of his own time. Donne was born a Catholic and became a Protestant. " On both sides ", wrote Gosse,[2] " he was sprung from Catholics of the staunch old stock, animated by a settled horror of reform, by a determination to oppose it." Donne had Catholicism in his blood and he did not find it easy to throw over the inherited habits and ways of feeling of innumerable generations. He himself was conscious of the difficulty. In 1615, only a few months after his ordination, he said in a remarkable letter to Sir Henry Godere :

" You shall seldom see a coyne, upon which the stamp were removed, though to imprint a better, but it looks awry and squint. And so for the most part do mindes which have received divers impressions."

From this we can turn to a famous sonnet written three years later :

Show me, deare Christ, thy Spouse, so bright and clear.
What ! is it She, which on the other shore
Goes richly painted ? Or which rob'd and tore
Laments and mournes in Germany and here ?
Sleepes she a thousand, then peepes up one year ?

---

[1] *Determinations*, p. 17.
[2] *Life and Letters of John Donne*, I., p. 4.

Is she selfe truth and errs ? now new, now outwore ?
Doth she, and did she, and shall she evermore
On one, on seaven, or on no hill appeare ?
Dwells she with us, or like adventuring knights
First travaile we to seeke and then make Love ?
Betray kind husband thy spouse to our sights,
And let myne amorous soule court thy mild Dove,
Who is most trew, and pleasing to thee, then
When she' is embrac'd and open to most men.

In speaking of Donne, we must remember that we
are dealing with a poet, with one in whom the dissen-
sions of the time were felt as an *experience* and were
never merely speculative questions. Donne's mind
was formed by a study of the great scholastics and I
believe that the secret of his work is the dramatic con-
flict between the intellectual and spiritual unity of the
middle ages and the spiritual multiplicity of the
Reformation. The Reformation was not something
that was going on in the outer world : it was a
spiritual struggle that was working itself out *inside* the
poet.

It should now be possible to draw conclusions.
When I said that the value of medieval literature lies
in its power of communicating *a feeling of stability and
confidence*, I was not forgetting that Dante lived in a
divided world and that Langland was Chaucer's con-
temporary. There was tension enough in the middle
ages and an instance nearer home—Hopkins—shows
us that Catholicism does not exclude tension, though
it might seem to in the writings of Claudel and Sigrid
Undset. We have to distinguish between writers who
were *outside* the tension and those who are *inside* it.
Beneath the clash recorded by Dante, beneath Villon's
lament for lost beauty and perhaps even the apparent
disunity of Hopkins, there is an underlying unity.
Their unrest is related to a background of harmony
in a way in which Donne's is not. With Donne we

meet perhaps for the first time, certainly in its most radical form, that divided self which is characteristic of modern poetry. In Hopkins, poet though he was of the age of Baudelaire, there is not the same kind of division, or rather the division and perplexity are related to something outside him which provides a solution and in a sense resolves the conflict. Donne's significance is different. He means so much to us because *he expresses for the first time the poet's awareness of living in an age of spiritual crisis*, and it is this that dominates nearly all the most important poetry written since him. The scene shifts, there are variations, apparent changes of emphasis, but at bottom the crisis is the same. Donne's work is more intense because he is at the point at which the break took place. The unity that was destroyed was real for him, not simply an inherited memory as it is for a contemporary poet.

IV

These inferences are reinforced by a study of Donne's method. Here his relations with scholasticism are illuminating. Donne was soaked in Aquinas, but though he borrows freely from scholastic terminology, he does so not in order to describe a common experience nor to enunciate metaphysical propositions. The language of the schools, the language of cultured Europe, which as Eliot has pointed out helped to make of Dante a European poet, becomes in Donne a private language to express Donne's own love experiences. His approach is very well brought out in the lines :

> In some close corner of my braine :
> There I enjoy and there kisse her,
> And so enjoy and so miss her.

What Donne did—and it is here that he is essentially

modern—was to dissociate *experience* from *things*. Life
no longer consists in doing something, in action. It
might just as well consist in sitting in one's study
analysing and speculating about one's own feelings.
Imagining takes the place of living. It is as good to
enjoy one's mistress in thought as in bed.

In one sense Donne increased the scope of poetry
enormously. His work is an intimate record of the
workings of consciousness, he is the forerunner of a
line of poets who have attempted to explore the whole
of the mind and to integrate it in poetry *unchecked by
any theological or metaphysical assumptions.* In his close-
ness to thought, in his power of expressing the simul-
taneous and often conflicting impulses of the mind, he
looks forward not simply to living poets, but to the
stream-of-consciousness novelists like Mrs. Woolf.
The Sunne Rising is a notable example.

> She'is all States, and all Princes, I,
> Nothing else is.
> Princes doe but play us ; compar'd to this,
> All honor's mimique ; All wealth alchimie.
> Thou sunne art halfe as happy'as wee,
> In that the world's contracted thus ;
> Thine age askes ease, and since thy duties bee
> To warme the world, that's done in warming us.
> Shine here to us, and thou art every where ;
> This bed thy center is, these walls, thy spheare.

Here the analysis of love, the sense that the whole
world is transfigured by human love and all else
nothing, is mingled with the fantastic reflections on
the contraction of the world and the sun's old age.

Donne's century was also the century of Descartes
and Spinoza, authors of the first modern treatises on
psychology. It does not seem unduly fanciful to hold
that the discoveries of these philosophers about the
'passions of the soul ' are paralleled by Donne's own

discoveries. *The Prohibition,* one of the best examples of his analytical power, is a good illustration.

> Yet, love and hate me too,
> So, these extreames shall neithers office doe ;
> Love mee, that I may die the gentler way ;
> Hate mee, because thy love is too great for mee ;
> Or let these two, themselves, not me decay ;
> So shall I, live, thy Stage, not triumph bee ;
> Lest thou thy love and hate and mee undoe,
> *To let mee live, O love and hate mee too.*

This passage reveals Donne's strength and his weakness. He is not simply reproducing Catullus's *odi et amo.* The poem, with its profound realisation of the interaction of love and hate, is a representative example of the way in which modern writers feel about love. We are already a long way from the simple though powerful desires of Chaucer's time : the mind is definitely being used to intensify the pleasure which comes through physical acts. It was against such an attitude, which was carried to its extreme limit by Marcel Proust, that the whole of D. H. Lawrence's writing was directed. Donne's strength, as seen in these lines, lies to a great extent in his psychological insight, in his power of analysing emotions and situations which is one of the heritages of a Catholic psychology. He is revealing human nature to itself in a new way.

It also reveals in a very striking way Donne's weakness. One of the effects of a Catholic psychology and a Catholic presentation of man is to guarantee a certain round of emotions. With a disappearance of these sanctions, however, the guarantee disappears too. The body of principles to which Donne should naturally, automatically relate experience has already grown blurred and dim. The poet no longer knows what love is ; he has burrowed so far into himself that he has got beyond all the traditional categories. Instead of trying to relate his particular experience to something outside it, he decomposes it into its component parts. It is whittled down to a balancing of the sensations of love and hate, or attraction and repulsion, against one another—anticipating, it seems to me, some of the more sensational findings of psycho-analysis. Thus Donne appears as the father of modern psychological poetry, of the unrelated analysis of emotion. He inaugurates the cult not of experience, which must always to some extent be the function of the poet, but of *unrelated* experience which becomes indistinguishable from a cult of sensation.

We can sum up Donne's contribution to poetry by saying that with him the intellect abandons its traditional rôle. For the middle ages the intellect was creative, was the principle of synthesis; for the moderns it tends to be the principle of destruction. It is no longer, as it had been for Dante, as it will be for Racine, the faculty of vision and synthesis; it is purely analytic. It is turned inward in order to analyse the poet's sensations without any attempt to organise or systematise them. Inevitably the intellect ends by destroying its own object, for in *The Prohibition* the analysis of emotion is pushed to the point at which emotion is destroyed.

v

It would serve no useful purpose to pursue the subsequent history of English poetry in detail. The position I am putting forward can be made clear by summarising the changes that have taken place in poetry since the middle ages. English poetry divides into three phases.

1. The medieval period when religion was an

integral part of everyday life and religion and poetry complementary.

2. The post-Renaissance period when there is a sharp division into religious and secular poetry. There are two main streams : the poetry of doubt and spiritual unrest on one side, and on the other a poetry which is religious in a very restricted sense. After Milton, there is no English *Christian* religious poet who can truly be considered a major poet until we come to Hopkins.[1]

3. The third period is the Romantic Movement, which is an attempt to build up a religious poetry on a basis which is completely independent of the Christian tradition. The poet becomes a seer and claims, in Shelley's words, to be regarded as one of the ' unacknowledged legislators of the world '.

The whole trend of significant contemporary poetry has been away from the Romantic Movement and back to the seventeenth century. The modern poet has taken over and developed the spiritual restlessness of Donne and his successors. But it would be a mistake to treat the Romantic Movement as something isolated and detached. For it was precisely the weaknesses that came into poetry at the Renaissance—an extreme individualism and an extreme subjectivism—that account for the failure of the Romantics.

The Romantic Movement had its origin in a genuine desire of God ; it was a genuine spiritual revolution caused by the fact that impulses, which had been driven underground and stifled in the eighteenth century, now demanded satisfaction. But instead of availing themselves of the resources of the great Western spiritual tradition, the Romantics rejected it

---

[1] There is, of course, the problematic figure of Blake. But it seems to me that Blake is too obscure and his experience too chaotic, for him to be regarded as a major poet in the full sense of the term.

entirely and the Movement ended inevitably in a thorough-going spiritual anarchy. The nature of the failure is apparent not only from the cloudy theology of the Romantic poets, but also from their inability to order their perceptions and translate them into words, which is one of the faculties of intellect. Nowhere is this more apparent than in the famous passage from the third book of the *Prelude* :

> To every natural form, rock, fruit or flower,
> Even the loose stones that cover the highway,
> I gave a moral life : I saw them feel,
> Or linked them to some feeling : the great mass
> Lay bedded in a quickening soul, and all
> That I beheld respired with inward meaning.

The tell-tale words are the repeated ' feel ' and ' feeling ', and curiously self-conscious phrases like ' moral life ', ' quickening soul ', ' inward meaning '. They are bad because they are blurred, because there is no longer any correspondence between the intellect and its object. The poet is unable to express what he feels and sees, and, instead, juggles with counters. He can only tell us vaguely that he does feel and does see.

Although this may seem at first sight to be remote from the criticism of Donne's use of intellect, in reality it is not. It simply marks the culminating stage in a process which sets in as soon as the mind turns away from *things* in order to concentrate on its own *reactions* to things. It means that feeling becomes completely divorced from things, as Wordsworth's feelings are really divorced from the flowers and the stones. The poet—it is a romantic trait—is simply exploiting the outer world in order to reveal fresh aspects of his own personality. From Wordsworth onwards, this tendency becomes more and more evident, and we witness the gradual submerging of the intellect in the emotions.

Finally, we have to estimate what poetry has gained and what it has lost by the break-up of Christendom. It would be absurd to deny that the human mind, and therefore poetry, has become in many respects subtler and more complex with the passing of time, even if the gifts have not always been made good use of. If modern poetry has lost that feeling of solidity and stability, at least it is richer and more varied, more profound in its knowledge of the human heart. The position has been well stated by Eliot in his essay on Dante :

" From the *Paradiso* ", he writes,[1] " [one learns] that more and more rarefied and remote states of beatitude can be the material for great poetry. And gradually we come to admit that Shakespeare understands a greater extent and variety of human life than Dante ; but that Dante understands deeper degrees of degradation and higher degrees of exaltation. . . . Shakespeare gives us the greatest *width* of human passion ; Dante the greatest altitude and greatest depth."

Mr. Eliot's distinction between the ' altitude ' and ' depth ' of Dante and the ' width ' of Shakespeare does not leave a great deal to add. The medievals were occupied in plotting the degrees of the spiritual life, the moderns with the complexity and variety of human passions. In none of the great Catholic poets, neither in Dante nor Chaucer, for all his insight, neither in Villon nor Racine, master psychologist though he was, nor in a prose-writer like Boccaccio, is there anything resembling the *psychological novelty* of the successors of Shakespeare and Donne. The loss is as clear as the gain. It is not merely that we have lost all that the close of the *Paradiso* means to us, that

[1] *Selected Essays*, pp. 238, 251.

other dimension added by Christianity; it is that there has been a breach between poetry and the Christian tradition.

The implications of this breach with the Christian tradition are very far reaching. I have already pointed out that nearly all Christian religious poetry written since Milton is minor poetry; but the matter does not finish there. The serious thing is that *all* religious poetry—the poetry of the great Romantics as well as of Herbert, Vaughan and Smart—becomes a special department of poetry. Instead of bringing the whole span of human existence within the poet's compass as it had done in the middle ages, religion seems to be turned against life and to have the effect of narrowing the poet's horizon. The conventional criticism of the Romantics—that there is a lack of human interest in their work—is only too true; and it is a criticism that applies to the greatest of them all, to Wordsworth, as much as to anyone. From whatever angle one looks at it, to be a religious poet in the modern world means to exclude a large part of life, as large a part as the unbelievers who leave out the supernatural altogether.

In the nineteenth century the processes inaugurated at the Renaissance reach their logical conclusion. The poet has no common outlook. He is completely deprived of the discipline provided by the Christian system and by the classic submission to things outside him. Thus the poets who were remarkable for their discoveries about the human mind like Donne, and the poets who were rich in religious intuitions like Wordsworth, failed alike to consolidate their findings and to integrate them into a scheme. They remained to a great extent unrelated experiences. The result is that the presentation of emotion grows more and more disorderly as the century progresses. The great difficulty of writing poetry at all in a civilisation like our own comes from the fact that the poet is faced with problems which could not arise in a healthy society. Instead of being able to use his powers *as a poet*, he is obliged to hunt for a fresh common outlook which is the only alternative to complete unintelligibility. This is illustrated by the work of W. H. Auden. There is no doubt that the author of *Poems* is possessed of natural endowments of the first order. What he might have achieved in a civilisation that gave him any help can only be a matter of conjecture. What happens in a civilisation that doesn't can be seen from his later work. It is a choice between the waste and confusion of *The Orators* and the impoverishment due to a materialist philosophy which is apparent in *The Dance of Death*.

The tragedy is that modern poets are cut off from their spiritual heritage. It has unfortunately been a matter of sheer gain and sheer loss, a failure to combine what was already there with what the modern poet had to add, or what he might have added, without relinquishing his heritage.

CHAPTER III

POETRY AND TRUTH

IN what has gone before I have tried to determine the relation between religion and poetry from the Catholic middle ages down to our own times. I have started from the assumption that all good art, whatever the beliefs on which it reposes, provides human nature with valuable experiences, though it can be seen that the value of the work may be altered by the beliefs which the poet holds at the time of writing. I have also suggested that European literature, generally speaking, can be divided into two periods. The first reflects the religious life of the race, even when not directly concerned with what is ordinarily understood by a religious subject. Its chief value seems to me to lie in the certainty and stability which are traceable to the beliefs behind it. It is this certainty, this belief in life, which disappears at the destruction of the old world, and in the second period we have a literature whose principal quality is to have expressed a sense of living in an age of spiritual crisis.

The result of the break-up of the old Europe, as we have seen, has been to divide culture into a vast number of tiny independent cells. A French writer distinguishes between the *universe* of the medieval poet and the *world* of the modern.[1] This distinction is a

---

[1] Mr. Middleton Murry as usual provides us with a convenient example. " His reaction to an episode ", he wrote of Hardy's poetry in *Aspects of Literature*, " has behind it and within it a reaction to the universe." The whole point is that Hardy did not react towards the *universe*, but towards the *world* created by Victorian materialists.

valid one. The medieval poet *was* dealing with the universe ; and when the middle ages came to an end we got instead a series of different worlds, each of them representing a partial and incomplete version of the universe. Every one of them has its own philosophy and its own poets, and the inhabitants base their lives on mutually exclusive and ultimately completely contradictory views of life.

From a cultural point of view, Catholicism is simply one of these ' worlds ' and this position has clearly created peculiar difficulties for the Catholic who writes poetry. What attitude should we expect a Catholic to take up towards the present situation ? All significant modern poetry must to some extent reflect the crisis through which we are passing, but it is clear that the approach of the Catholic will be different from one who is writing from a non-religious point of view. Mr. Leavis has said that poetry should express " a modern sensibility, the ways of feeling, the modes of experience, of one fully alive in his own time ". For our own purposes, we can modify this to " the ways of feeling, the modes of experience, of *a Catholic* fully alive in his own time ". Catholic poetry therefore should not be concerned exclusively with the difficulties of a Catholic living in a secularised society. It should be concerned with the *common* difficulties of contemporary man ; but, given an equal poetic endowment, it ought of course to be more satisfactory *as poetry* than the work of the non-religious writer because the Catholic still has behind him a whole and coherent philosophy where other writers have none. It must be pointed out, however, that poetry which is religious in the full sense can only be written in a Christian society. This does not mean a society in which there are a large number of Christians or even a country whose government is officially Catholic. It means a society whose outlook as a whole is based on Christian principles and whose life is in the widest sense religious. In the present state of society we must expect to find instead a poetry such as Hopkins', which is primarily concerned with the vicissitudes of the interior life and which necessarily leaves certain aspects of the present situation out of account.

It is, perhaps, because Catholics who write poetry and Catholics who write novels have never sufficiently considered their position that so little significant Catholic literature has been written. Modern Catholic writers on the whole have been of two kinds. They have either been religious in the restricted sense described in the previous chapter, or they have made the mistake of trying to write the sort of poetry that can only be written in a Catholic society. It is unfortunate that they should have assumed that Catholicism is bound up with a rigid unchanging outlook which is independent of current events. For this has created an *historical* attitude towards the Faith which prevents a writer from being " fully alive in his own age " and which is necessarily sterile. Claudel, for example, is as firmly grounded in his faith as Dante, but there is a world of difference between *The Divine Comedy* and *The Satin Slipper*. It is impossible to go straight against the spirit of the age or to achieve *complete* immunity from it, and no great writer would ever attempt it. Claudel does not suffer from the modern unrest, he is outside the tension ; but one feels moved to conclude that he is ' outside the tension ' in an unfavourable sense and that there is a curious hollowness about his most celebrated work. Indeed, his most successful poetry is neither *The Satin Slipper* nor *L'annonce faite à Marie*, but the *Cinq grandes odes*, where he is more in touch with the present age, more aware of its difficulties. A similar criticism has,

I think, to be made of another distinguished writer
—a novelist this time—who appears at first to be
the antithesis of Claudel, François Mauriac. There
is tension enough in Mauriac, but it is difficult not
to feel that this tension is in a curious way artificial,
voulu ; that his Jansenism is as much an imposed
attitude as Claudel's medievalism.

I am not, however, primarily concerned with the
problems of the Catholic poet in secularist society,
but to establish a general theory of poetry and truth.
We have, I think, to begin with an admission. I have
already said at the beginning of this essay that our
" appreciation of a poet's emotions involves an appre-
ciation of his valuations which may be highly per-
verse ". It is true that much of what is valuable in
Dante is due to the fact that his view of the universe
is the true one, and that some of the shortcomings of
Eliot's earlier work are traceable to a distorted con-
ception of reality. But in spite of theoretical diffi-
culties, the fact remains that we do derive valuable
experiences from a poet whose work may present a
view of the universe which in some cases is incom-
plete and in others probably wrong. What we have
to explain is the enormous attraction that the author
of the *Fleurs du mal* or *The Waste Land* may have for
the Catholic, which is certainly not a thing that can
be dismissed in terms of æsthetic enjoyment.

In a passage in his masterly essay on ' Tradition and
Individual Talent ', Eliot remarks :

" No poet, no artist of any art, has complete
meaning alone. His significance, his appreciation is
the appreciation of his relation to the dead poets and
artists. . . . The necessity that he shall conform, that
he shall cohere, is not one-sided. What happens when
a new work of art is created is something that happens
simultaneously to all the works of art which preceded

it. The existing monuments form an ideal order among themselves which is modified by the introduction of the new (the really new) work of art among them. The existing order is complete before the new work arrives ; for order to persist after the supervention of novelty, the *whole* existing order must be, if ever so slightly, altered, and so the relation, proper tone, value of each work of art towards the whole are readjusted, and this is conformity between the old and the new." [1]

The really important point in this passage is the assertion that the great poet is not an individual, but a member of a hierarchy of dead and living poets. *Thus the experience we get from major poetry is not something that happened to an individual, it is something that happened to human nature.* And this has been most brilliantly put by the poet Hopkins in one of his letters :

" There have been in all history a few, a very few men, whom common repute, even where it did not trust them, has treated as having had something happen to them that does not happen to other men, as having *seen something*, whatever that really was. Plato is the most famous of these. Or to put it as it seems to me that I must somewhere have written to you or to somebody, *human* nature in these men saw something, got a shock ; wavers in opinion looking back, whether there was anything in it or not, but is in a tremble ever since. Now what Wordsworthians mean is what would seem to be the growing mind of the English-speaking world at large, is that in Wordsworth, when he wrote, our human nature got another of those shocks, and the tremble from it is spreading." [2]

[1] *Selected Essays*, p. 15.
[2] Letter to R. W. Dixon, October 10th, 1886, in *Letters*, I., O.U.P., 1935.

Hopkins was of course referring to some special kind of experience or ' shock ', but what he said is equally true of most of the great poets of all time. In them " our human nature . . . saw something ". That is the whole point. There must, as Eliot insisted, be continuity throughout the ages, and this continuity is guaranteed by the constant factor in our human nature. The human mind develops and changes, experience varies and new experiences are discovered ; but identity persists, there is always some measure of communication possible between all ages and all civilisations. We know from experience that through some modification of sensibility the literature of some past age or some other civilisation suddenly becomes very much more accessible to us than it has been before. It is continuity in this sense that I have stressed in speaking of Tradition. Now if a major poem is something that happens to human nature, it must happen to us all ; whatever our beliefs we cannot remain unaffected by it ; whether Catholics or not, we are bound to be affected by what happened to our human nature in Shakespeare or in Baudelaire. This, it seems to me, is why we can and do find value in writers whose outlook is the antithesis of the Catholic outlook.

What needs to be emphasised is that modern literature marks a great and growing breach between human nature at its highest and the European Tradition. These experiences are happening to people who are outside the Church, and therefore to a large extent cut off from a man's common spiritual heritage. Now when a great writer is in this position he often comes after a time to a standstill. He is deprived of the supernatural, and as soon as his talent is exhausted he dries up, as Wordsworth dried up. There is only repetition and sterility left—the sort of sterility we find in the later work of Proust, Joyce and Virginia Woolf. Nor is it confined to the masters. Even the best of our younger poets, Auden, Bottral and Empson, show signs of the same tendency after their first work.

CHAPTER IV

THE LIBERAL CRITIC

'THE trouble with English criticism', a distinguished French critic, M. Charles Du Bos, once said, 'is that it is cut off from the spiritual life of the race.' It is clear that if we are to have an effective criticism, it must be based on permanent standards. Without a metaphysic there can be no relation between the different writers, or between the value represented for us by Chaucer, Dante, Shakespeare, Racine, Baudelaire, Hopkins and Eliot. They are in danger of becoming superb but unrelated experiences and there is no really satisfactory method of assessing their importance for us.

It is precisely a system of this sort that has been lacking in England since the eighteenth century. The eighteenth century recognised the need for some permanent standard and formulated the metaphysical concept of 'Nature'. This may not have been altogether adequate, but whatever its shortcomings it did act as a corrective and was the foundation of the intellectual élite which existed at the time. It gave us the 'common reader' to whom Johnson could appeal. Since the break-up of the reading public and the final dissolution of eighteenth-century standards, the one attempt to put criticism on a philosophical basis has been made by Coleridge; but Coleridge was himself the victim of conflicting philosophical systems and was partially submerged in the mists of German idealism. His contribution to criticism is far more that of a psychologist than of a metaphysician. It thus happens that while English criticism has been rich in critical aperçus, it has been of comparatively little assistance to the artist and has done practically nothing to stem the tide of cultural disintegration or the break-up of tradition.

The consequences of the rapid decline of metaphysics since the time of Coleridge have occupied English critics a good deal. A number of attempts have been made to provide literary criticism with a system and to determine the proper function of poetry, though no satisfactory solution has so far emerged. In this chapter and in the chapters which follow I wish to examine some of the proposed solutions. The three critics discussed in the present chapter are described as ' Liberals ' to distinguish them from critics who must be called ' dogmatic '. For in spite of his preoccupation with psychology and his insistence on Science, a writer like Dr. Richards is essentially a lonely individualist and the equation in the last analysis a personal one. It is perhaps necessary to add that for the purpose of this essay I am obliged to concentrate on a single aspect of the three writers discussed here and that what is said about that aspect is not intended as a reflection on their other work, for which I have considerable admiration.

MIDDLETON MURRY

Mr. Middleton Murry's work has been to try to find a religious basis for literary criticism, and his essay ' Literature and Religion ' in *To the Unknown God* is perhaps the most striking illustration of the modern tendency to make literature a substitute for religion.

" Literature ", writes Mr. Murry, " which is a manifestation of that same soul whose deepest anatomy is contained in religion, must inevitably be knit up with, be indissolubly bound to, religion. There

44

is no escape. Religion and literature are branches of the same everlasting root." [1]

Mr. Murry makes his principal argument the historical relation between religion and literature before and after the Renaissance. He finds it

" so close and unbreakable that in those periods of human history when religion is superbly organised and close to its own living centre, the creative impulse in literature might well be enfeebled because the need it satisfies is less urgent. Perhaps the coincidence of the time when the spiritual and temporal realities of the Christian Church seemed identical and the time when western literature was moribund is not in the least fortuitous ; and it may be that the decay of dogmatic religion, because of its failure to express the religious reality and satisfy the religious needs of the soul, is a necessary condition in order that literature may truly grow and flourish. It may be that the moment comes when the most sensitive minds are compelled to be of the Church, but not in it : when precisely because they are profoundly religious they are bound to work in complete independence of what passes for religion in their day." [2]

This statement is a curious mixture of true fact and false inference. In the first place, it is not altogether fair to attribute the comparative poverty of medieval literature to the dominance of organised religion. There were strong historical reasons for it. It must be remembered that medieval society was in many respects a primitive one and illiteracy widespread. Latin was still the language of cultured Europe and the work of poets in the vernacular still a comparatively rare thing. Moreover, there were strong prejudices against poetry as distinct from the ' useful

[1] *To the Unknown God*, pp. 163–4.
[2] *Ibid.*, pp. 164–5.

arts', as we know from the efforts of Renaissance critics to justify poetry on moral grounds. In the second place, Mr. Murry forgets that whatever its form in other parts of Europe, the Renaissance in Spain was Christian and brought with it a Christian literary revival of which one of the greatest names was St. John of the Cross. Nor must we forget that in our own country ' the continuity of English prose ' was preserved by religious writers like Hilton, Juliana of Norwich and the anonymous author of *The Cloud of Unknowing* whose works reveal a splendid combination of spiritual insight and artistic sensibility.[1]

Still, since medieval literature was small in output and the decline of Christendom followed by a great literary outburst, it seems probable that in the middle ages something went into religion which afterwards found an outlet in poetry. One might put it that the whole of medieval sensibility was incorporated in medieval religion.[2] In the middle ages the religious life was so complete that the whole life of the individual, the life of the senses as well as the intellect, was absorbed in it. The medieval did not feel to the same extent the modern writer's need for self-expression : instead he expressed himself by taking part in the life of the community.

This, of course, is not the ' close and unbreakable ' relation envisaged by Mr. Murry.

" We may go even farther than this ", he writes, " and declare that the originating experience of any truly creative work of literature, however small, is in some measure and perhaps essentially religious. That recognition by the writer of his theme, that delighted apprehension of his material in the world outside him or within, seems to be nothing else than the sudden

---

[1] *Cf.* R. W. Chambers, *The Continuity of English Prose*, p. 115.
[2] *Cf.* Rémy de Gourmont, *Le problème du style*, pp. 48–9, 107.

perception that an immaterial and all-pervading essence can be contained in a single symbol. What is perceived is perceived as something much greater than is apprehended in and through the particular." [1]

This position has since been consolidated by a remarkable paper on ' The Metaphysic of Poetry ' in *Countries of the Mind, II.*

" The essential condition of philosophical poetry ", writes Murry, " is that the poet should believe that there is a faculty of mind superior to the poetic : that was possible for Dante, tremendous poet though he was : but since Shakespeare lived and wrote it is not possible. Shakespeare created a new order of values independent of the great medieval Christian tradition, yet spiritual through and through : a system of values, so far as we can see, completely divorced from any faith in immortality or after justice, compatible, indeed, with a real agnosticism, yet in height and breadth of the word profoundly religious." [2]

In these passages we have again to distinguish between true fact and false inference. The significant words are " Shakespeare created a new order of values " and the assertion that we can no longer believe that " there is a faculty of mind superior to the poetic ", which is tantamount to saying that metaphysics has definitely been superseded by poetry. It is certainly true that minds which might otherwise have concerned themselves with metaphysical thinking were driven into poetry by the break-up of the medieval Christian tradition. It is also true that post-Renaissance poetry has at times assumed a speculative aspect. What strikes me as false is the assumption that the poetic faculty is superior to the intellectual as a means of *knowledge*, and that the function of the

[1] *Op. cit.*, p. 188.
[2] *Countries of the Mind, II.*, pp. 58–9.

metaphysician not only can, but ought to be exercised by the poet. We are thrown back on the scholastic distinction : the object of intellect is truth and that of art the beautiful, though what we mean by the beautiful in this context needs to be carefully defined. It is clear that the poet is exceeding his function when he sets out to provide us with a ' philosophy ' or an ' order of values ', though he has been forced into this by the decay of metaphysics. To write of Shakespeare " creating an order of values . . . independent of the great medieval Christian tradition " means that Shakespeare rejected the Christian tradition. In short, the Christian is faced with a poetry which derives its power from the fact that it is based on a conception of reality which he is bound to regard as incomplete ; and the intensity, the tension, of modern poetry is closely connected with its incompleteness.

The misunderstandings in Mr. Murry's pronouncements make it essential to distinguish between religion and art. Religion and art are both activities ; they are both connected with a specific kind of experience. Religion is the duty that we as creatures pay to God whose existence and attributes are known through the exercise of reason and through Revelation. The practice of religion may be accompanied by an experience which we commonly describe as ' religious experience ', but this is by no means always the case. Art, on the other hand, is not immediately concerned with God or with speculations about the nature of the universe. It is the imaginative interpretation of the world as given in sense-experience ; its origin is neither in mysticism nor in speculation, but in the organisation of sense-perceptions—though we know from the work of writers like St. John of the Cross, Vaughan and Hopkins that the religious life may be expressed in poetry. What we often have then in both cases is an experience supervening upon an activity ; but since the two activities differ considerably there seems to me to be no ground at all for assuming a similarity in the accompanying experience. Indeed, Mr. Murry's attitude appears to involve a confusion between two distinct orders of experience. What right have we to assume identity ? There is, of course, the misleading epiphenomenal resemblance between the accompanying experiences. But against this there is the theologian's contention that mystical experience is a form of *knowledge*. God is known without the intermediary of a concept. It has been argued that poetic experience is also a form of knowledge, and that the poet's object is known immediately without the intermediary of a concept. But even supposing this to be true, there would only be analogy and not identity between the experiences. For in this case the *objects* of the two activities would be the only basis for distinction and they are not the same. The object of religious experience is a transcendental one, but the object of art very seldom is.

If Mr. Murry uses the word ' religious ' in the sense of mystical experience in the passages given above, he also uses it in a somewhat different sense in others. In another part of the same essay, for instance, he tells us that literature since the Renaissance " is the record of the soul's struggle after life and God ".[1]

" Literature is become the great religious adventure of the human soul simply because it affords the only complete expression to the adventuring human soul, and the human soul is bound upon an adventure which is necessarily religious. . . ."[2]

This use of the word religious seems to me to be

[1] *To the Unknown God*, p. 170.
[2] *Ibid.*, pp. 191-2.

arbitrary and in a way negative. It may be true that literature since the Renaissance " is the record of the soul's struggle after life and God " ; but if it is, it can only be a struggle for something which the middle ages possessed and which the modern world has lost. It is a case of recognising facts. What is deepest in modern literature is a sense of loss, and over this loss Mr. Murry is rejoicing and calling it a religious loss.

What is valuable in Mr. Murry's discussion is the insistence on the close relation between religion and poetry. It must be remembered, however, that religion is not like art the expression of human nature, but the constant factor which determines human nature. Thus we must distinguish between poetry which reflects the spiritual life of the race as Dante, Chaucer, Langland, Racine and Hopkins may be said to reflect it, and literature which is certainly a substitute for religion as, in some measure, it was a substitute with Shelley, Keats, Wordsworth and the Romantic Revival generally. For poetry to be religious does not mean, as Mr. Murry recognises, that it must be devotional : it simply means that it reflects something given to it by religion.

Mr. Murry's view that the full flowering of the poetic spirit depends on the disintegration of organised religion is therefore only true when applied to special periods like the Romantic Revival. It is noticeable that though the Romantic Revival in England and France started as a protest against the petrifaction of organised religion and from a genuine desire for God, it became in fact a substitute for religion with a new mythology of its own.

" At this time ", wrote Jacques Rivière [1] of the Romantic Revival in France, " At this time, literature

---

[1] *Nouvelle Revue Française*, February, 1924, p. 161.

took over the heritage of religion and modelled itself on the thing it was replacing. The writer had become a priest, literature the host which it was his function to consecrate."

I. A. RICHARDS

It is well known that when properly applied, psychology may render considerable services to the study of literature. Unfortunately, however, the psychologist is inclined to forget that psychology is only one of the departmental sciences and to try to explain everything in terms of empirical psychology. For our own purposes Richards is chiefly interesting as an instance of what happens when one tries to construct a ' philosophy ' which is based on an inadequate view of the nature of man.

For Richards (as for Francis Bacon) the poet is important because he has experiences which are denied to the general run of mankind and he is also able to communicate them to a reader. This is perfectly obvious, but when we ask *why* the poet's experience is valuable we at once find ourselves in difficulties. According to Richards, poetry provides us with the most valuable experience ; and the most valuable experience we could wish for a hypothetical friend would be :

" One in which as much as possible of himself is engaged (as many of his impulses as possible). And this with as little conflict, as little mutual interference between different sub-systems of his activities as there can be. The more he lives and the less he thwarts himself the better. That briefly is our answer as psychologists, as outside observers abstractly describing the state of affairs. And if it is asked, what does such a life feel like, how is it to live through ? The answer is that it feels like and is the experience of poetry." [1]

[1] *Science and Poetry*, p. 33.

We know that poetry is an increase of *being*. Richards has done no more than re-state the Aristotelian theory in the language of the modern psychologist. But an Aristotelian can ' discriminate between experiences ' and ' evaluate them ' [1] (Richards' definition of the function of criticism) because he bases his enquiry on a general theory of the nature of man. He knows that man is capable of ' higher ' and ' lower ' experiences and that life is not, as Richards appears to think, a matter of satisfying ' as many of his impulses as possible '. Thus the distinction of the one is *qualitative* and of the other purely *quantitative*. It is a little curious, then, that Richards, after putting forward this theory, should proceed to attack the philosophical basis on which it rests.

" It may seem odd ", he writes, " that we do not more definitely make the thoughts the rulers and causes of the rest of the experience. To do just this has been in fact the grand error of traditional psychology. Man prefers to stress the features which distinguish him from monkey and chief among these are his intellectual capacities. Important though they are, he has given them a rank to which they are not entitled. Intellect is an adjunct to the interests, a means by which they adjust themselves more successfully. *Man is not in any sense primarily an intelligence ; he is a system of interests*. Intelligence helps man but does not run him." [2]

It is clear from this passage that Richards' psychology derives from the bad tradition that came into being in the eighteenth century and was developed during the nineteenth. It is frankly a survival of a rationalism in which no one any longer believes. Few

---

[1] *The Principles of Literary Criticism*, 2nd edit., London, 1926, p. 4.
[2] *Science and Poetry*, p. 21. (Italics mine.)

reputable psychologists would subscribe to the dictum that man is nothing but ' a system of interests ' ; the best psychologists indeed are returning to an Aristotelian position and emphasise the existence of a rational soul.

The attempt to reduce man to ' a system of interests ' raises insuperable difficulties for the critic. For if man is simply a shifting changing ' system of interests ' it is difficult to see how there can be any fundamental identity through the ages. There can be no constant factor in human nature nor even a single prevailing interest. Man is reduced to ' a bundle of perceptions ' which are largely determined by environment. This makes any permanent standards unthinkable, for those experiences in which ' as much as possible ' of man's self was ' engaged ' in medieval times appear to Richards to be the merest moonshine, and, one supposes, largely valueless in helping modern man to organise his impulses. This seems to be Richards' view. Contemporary poetry, as he rightly insists, ' must have sprung in part from the contemporary situation '. But when Richards speaks of ' the contemporary situation ' he does not mean that poetry must simply reflect the crisis through which we are passing ; he means that it must reflect his own personal attitude which is based on the supposed destruction of traditional beliefs by science. Thus he can tell us that :

" Over whole tracts of natural emotional responses we are to-day like dahlias whose sticks have been removed. And the effect of the neutralisation of nature is only in its beginnings. Consider the probable effects upon love poetry in the near future of the kind of enquiry into basic human constitution exemplified by psycho-analysis.

" A sense of desolation, of uncertainty, of futility,

of the groundlessness of aspiration, of the vanity of endeavour and a thirst for the life-giving water which seems suddenly to have failed, are the signs of the consciousness of this necessary reorganisation of our lives." [1]

That one claiming to write as a scientist should be guilty of this miserable piece of sentimentality is not, perhaps, of great moment. But it does matter that a complete misunderstanding of first principles (as shown, for instance, in the pathetic faith in psycho-analysis) should lead to a drastic impoverishment of poetry by shutting it off from whole regions of experience which were once of the highest value.

The ' life-giving water ', for which Dr. Richards thirsts, is a somewhat strange elixir.

" By effecting a complete severance between his poetry and *all* beliefs, and this without any weakening of the poetry, he (T. S. Eliot) has realised what might otherwise have remained largely a speculative possibility, and has shown the way to the only solution of these difficulties." [2]

This last statement has been vigorously denied by Eliot, which seems to prove that Richards' criterion is a purely personal one. He projects his own senti-mental attitude into the poem and then praises it for showing the way out of our difficulties. Poetry, he adds, " is capable of saving us ; it is a perfectly pos-sible means of overcoming chaos". But if poetry itself reflects the modern chaos, how can it overcome it ? It is a strange attempt to make poetry a substitute for religion. We can agree that those experiences are most valuable which bring as much as possible of man's nature into play, but it would be absurd to

[1] *Op. cit.*, p. 64.
[2] *Op. cit.*, pp. 64–5.

pretend that the poetry of negation and retreat which Richards holds up for our admiration can possibly compensate anybody for what has been lost in order to make it possible.

The mass of contradictions in which Richards involves himself is revealed in his final pronouncement. When he speaks of freeing man " from the entanglement with belief which now takes from poetry half its power and would then take all ", he is creating a hopeless opposition between literature and life. The only justification for literature is that it does increase our appreciation of life which in one way or another it reflects. It is true that contemporary poetry expresses the absence of belief, but a poetry which is by definition *incapable* of expressing the religious life and which in fact depends for its existence on the decay of that life is hopelessly inadequate and is parasitic on the life it pretends to express.

One cannot leave Richards without a word about the famous discussion of ' Poetry and Beliefs ' which took place some years ago. It is closely connected with the different problems with which this essay deals.

It was discovered by certain critics that they still enjoyed the work of religious poets like Donne and Hopkins, though they no longer held the beliefs which were the very heart of their poetry. They then asked whether it was necessary to share the beliefs of the writer during a reading of the poem in order to enjoy it to the full. It was generally admitted that if one shared the poet's beliefs one got more out of the poem ; but it was argued that this was not absolutely *necessary* on the ground that during the reading of the poem the question of the truth or falsity of the statements it contained did not arise. One simply participated in the poet's emotion.

This theory seems to me to contain some truth and

a good deal of error. It is, of course, true that one can enjoy the poet's mastery of language and to some extent share his feelings without sharing his views. But it is plain that it is not merely a question of degree, of getting more or less out of a poem. If we share Dante's beliefs as a poet, our experience in reading his poem will be *different* from the experience of a person to whom Dante's theology and philosophy are moonshine. Richards' view overlooks the fact that in many cases the beliefs were an organic part of the poet's experience and that in writing *he did assume that they were shared by his audience*.[1] But to argue, as Eliot does, that a Catholic is in a better position to appreciate *The Divine Comedy* simply because he is better *instructed* than the outsider, is to weaken the matter to an unnecessary extent. The poet assumed not instruction, but positive belief. It seems to me that a reader who definitely rejects the belief in a fixed order, which we find in Dante's poetry,[2] will simply be filled with a sense of nostalgia, of longing after a vanished dream, which naturally changes the whole nature of the original experience.

What I wish to do here is to state the same problem from a different angle, from the angle of the Catholic in face of a secularist literature. As Catholics we are continually reading writers to whom our deepest beliefs are either survivals or rank superstition. The point I wish to make is already suggested in Richards' theory of poetry and beliefs. Richards apparently holds the view that there is no essential difference between our ordinary emotions and those we receive from poetry, except that the poet's are richer and better organised. Now it seems to me that for once

---

[1] This point was first made to me by Fr. M. C. D'Arcy, S.J., in the course of a conversation some years ago.
[2] See pp. 13–19 above.

the German æstheticians are right and that we must assume—as I think Richards unconsciously assumes—some sort of ' æsthetic emotion '. We have the experience, but we are all the time aware that it is an illusion. There is in every one of us a *natural* desire for ' all experience '. We are thus enabled by means of poetry to come in contact with minds which are as remote from our own as they can well be. This may sound as though I am rejecting Richards' theory when applied to religious poetry and re-stating it to suit myself. This is not the case. With Richards, there is a positive belief to be disposed of; in our own, simply an absence of belief. What is true of both is that the experience of the poem is in a sense an illusion ; but the main point is that when associated with positive belief, as Dante's poetry is, poetry undoubtedly has quite a different kind of reality for us, a reality which remains after reading the poem. It is emotion leading the intellect to the perception and realisation of truths about the universe. The work of an unbeliever, of one whose work assumes no beliefs, does not present a picture of the universe which we as Catholics must reject. It is not bound up with a dogmatic atheism. It simply presents a series of moods which are largely unrelated and into which Catholics can enter like anyone else. Such poetry is capable of telling us a good deal about the state of the writer and the society in which he lives. In this sense it is certainly ' a mine of practical truth '. If I have understood him rightly, it was this kind of truth that Lawrence had in mind in his definition of the function of art given in the first chapter.

F. R. LEAVIS

Like Richards, Mr. Leavis is concerned over the state of contemporary culture ; but though he believes

that poetry matters, he is too sensible to attribute to
it the magical qualities with which Richards (following
Arnold) is inclined to invest it. Mr. Leavis's parti-
cular task, however, has been to insist on the impor-
tance of literary criticism. The strength of his position
is his conviction that the literary critic has an impor-
tant function to perform in contemporary society and
to have shown what that function is. We have come
to see that poetry is one of the most reliable indications
of the condition of culture at a given time, and that
criticism of poetry is in fact criticism of culture.

" Literary criticism ", wrote Mr. Leavis in the pre-
face to a collection of essays called *Determinations*, " is
concerned with more than literature. . . . A serious
interest in literature cannot be merely literary . . . it
is likely to be drawn from a perception of—what must
be a preoccupation with—the problems of social
equity and order and of cultural health."
" We take it as axiomatic ", wrote the editors of
Scrutiny in their first number, " that concern for the
standards of living implies concern for the standards
in the arts."

This is a salutary reminder, but there would have
been nothing remarkable about these pronouncements
had the matter been allowed to rest there. What is
remarkable is the fact that Mr. Leavis's approach to
literature has been a strictly literary one and that he
has managed to make criticism do something fresh.
What is permanently valuable in his work is its con-
creteness. The minute analysis of words and language,
which is characteristic of Cambridge criticism, has
appeared to some to be a pedantic game. In fact, it
is precisely through a study of a writer's style that the
critic is able to get at the state of mind behind the
work. It is impossible for anyone who is familiar
with the best work that has appeared in *Scrutiny* not

to be struck by the way in which the field of criticism has been enlarged. It is not merely that the instruments of criticism have been improved—it is that the findings of modern criticism would have been entirely outside the scope of literary criticism a few years ago. This does not mean that literary criticism can perform the work of the theologian or of the philosopher. Criticism is one of the departmental sciences, but where a writer is concerned it is the literary critic who provides the philosopher with his data. Thus the question whether *Lady Chatterley's Lover*, objectively considered, is or is not a healthy book, is not one which can be settled out of hand by the theologian. It can only be determined by a study of the language in which it is written. A study of this sort is purely technical and can only be undertaken by the trained critic. My point is that though criticism can never be a substitute for metaphysics, neither can metaphysics be a substitute for literary criticism.

Inevitably Mr. Leavis has had to do a good deal of scavenging, and much of his writing has been a polemic against the general levelling down represented by Book Society Choice, Priestley novels and Arnold Bennett criticism. The emotions, as we know, can either lead the intellect to realise truth in a fresh way, or can equally well lead to the complete disorganisation of the intellectual life. Since this is so, we must admire the concern shown by Mr. Leavis for the emotional life and the exacting standards he applies. When we come to ask what he has to offer in the way of a constructive policy, it is less easy to follow him. There is a plea for an organised cultured minority— people who are concerned for ' the standards of living ' and ' the standards in the arts '. It is rightly argued that in the long run an élite of this kind would act as a leaven. It is true that much could be done in this way, but is it enough ? Personally I hardly think so. Moreover, there seems to be a dangerous admiration in some of Mr. Leavis's writings for the eighteenth century when these conditions actually existed ; but it must be remembered that the eighteenth century was really the last phase of the old order, and owed its stability ultimately to traditional sanctions which Mr. Leavis no longer accepts. Indeed, I sometimes feel that he is trying to revive the conditions without the sanctions on which they were based.

In one of the essays in *For Continuity*, Mr. Leavis remarks that " the recovery of religious sanctions in some form seems necessary to the health of the world ". Not the least of Mr. Leavis's services is to have drawn attention to the dilemma of modern criticism, to have asserted the need of a system though he has not himself been able to provide that system.[1] The problem is not one that is likely to be solved easily. I cannot pretend to offer anything like a final solution in this essay, though I shall try in a later chapter to state the attitude of the Catholic towards it.

What must our final estimate be ? It seems to me that anyone seriously interested in literature must feel gratitude to Mr. Leavis for the way in which he has improved the instruments of criticism which is the first step towards the solution of the problem before us. His insistence on words and rhythm as the critic's starting point is undoubtedly right, but the experience which emerges from the analysis must itself be related to something beyond it, must be integrated into some sort of scheme. The absence of a scheme means that the critic stops short and is inclined to escape into a world of words and verbal analysis. The sort of difficulty that the critic encounters can be seen most

---

[1] See *Scrutiny* for June, 1936, pp. 88–9, for a good statement of his position.

clearly by a comparison between Mr. Leavis's admirable studies of Swift [1] and Wordsworth [2] and the less satisfactory studies of ' English Poetry in the Seventeenth Century ' and ' English Poetry in the Eighteenth Century '.[3] He has no difficulty in isolating what is valuable in the experience of an individual writer, but is less successful when he comes to discuss a period or a movement. When he refers in one place, for example, to " the great changes that came over English civilisation in the seventeenth century " and leaves it at that, it is difficult not to feel that vital problems are being overlooked and that the discussion of technique is preventing the critic from perceiving the issues involved.

[1] V. *Determinations*, London, 1934.
[2] V. *Revaluation*, London, 1936.
[3] Reprinted in *Revaluation* as ' The Line of Wit ' and ' The Augustan Tradition '.

CHAPTER V

THE MARXIST CRITIC

"To tell the truth, literature is never happy for long without a master; it needs a settled background. Even now it is trying to decide which master to serve—the revolutionary mass-movement or the liberalism of Freud." (C. Day Lewis.)

AMONG the welter of conflicting 'philosophies' which divide the contemporary world, Marxism stands out as a conscientious attempt to provide a system that will take the whole of life into account. Marxists themselves attach so much importance to the arts and have given them such prominence in their scheme of social reconstruction, that no discussion of the place of poetry in life would be complete which did not say something of their work. The Marxist theory of art has, indeed, a peculiar relevance to the present discussion. It is a reaction against the tendency to turn poetry into a substitute for religion; but in their anxiety to restore art to its proper place in the life of the community, Marxists have made it the slave of a narrow ideology and deprived it of that freedom without which there can be no art.

It is not surprising that Marxism should have appealed so strongly to many of our younger writers. It is clear from literary history that it is easier to write well in an age dominated by a common outlook than in an age in which there is none. Writers turn to Marxism in the hope that an initial act of faith in its tenets will provide a solution to their æsthetic problems and a framework in which they can express their personal vision instead of being compelled to waste their talents in working out a fresh philosophy. Although one may find the Marxist position unsatisfactory, it would be unfair to pretend that Marxists have made no contribution to the problems of art. Marxist critics have undoubtedly drawn attention to points which have been overlooked by other critics and in this way have succeeded in clarifying many of the issues involved.

What is most valuable in the Marxist approach is its insistence on the social factor in art, on the fact that literature can only be truly healthy when it is the expression of the life of the community as an undivided whole. Now the literature of the last 200 years reflects for the most part the disintegration of the social unit. The work of Fielding, for example, though in no sense the product of a ' classless society ', was based on an outlook which was common to all classes and which indeed transcended class distinctions ; and that gives his work, in spite of certain obvious limitations, a strength of its own, a strength which the modern novel has lost. Fielding's outlook was neither as profound nor as comprehensive as Chaucer's, but it was undoubtedly based on that ' blood connection ' which, as D. H. Lawrence acutely pointed out, had disappeared by the time we reach Jane Austen. When the artist lost contact with the people, something vital went out of his art. It is not merely that modern literature is individualist, an art for the élite : it is rather that excessive analysis is gradually destroying its object. Human nature is defaced, and the quality of the art suffers in consequence. The sort of change that is taking place can be appreciated by comparing the Wife of Bath's Prologue with Mrs. Bloom's monologue at the close of Joyce's *Ulysses*, *Tom Jones* with parts of *The Rainbow*.

The work of both Joyce and Lawrence is notable for its attempt to restore natural human nature to its proper position, to restore to art something that has been lost by excessive cerebration. But the attempt failed. Compared with Chaucer and Fielding human nature in Joyce and Lawrence is warped and stunted. The solidarity behind Chaucer and Fielding was conserved by the whole structure of the social organism and once it was lost it could not be recovered by the methods they employed.

At the present time, therefore, as Marxists point out, the world is divided into two main groups : ' the bourgeois ' and ' the proletariat '. Art and culture are practically the monopoly of the bourgeois and, as we all admit, the art which most clearly reflects the crisis through which we are passing has been produced by this class—while the proletariat has ceased to produce anything at all. We must also admit that for all its refinement, this art has become exceedingly precarious, an art of disillusion and despair. It is clear that this state cannot continue indefinitely. The middle classes have been living on their intellectual capital for some time and there are unmistakable signs that it is nearing exhaustion. The problem which faces not only Marxists, but also all who are concerned for the future of civilisation is the blending of these two opposites. Marxists believe that it can only be accomplished through social revolution and the creation of the classless society, and that all writers who are worthy of the name ought to devote their energies to this work. It is certainly evident from the experiments of Joyce and Lawrence that this can only be brought about by a complete transformation of existing society, by a veritable change in human nature.

" A writer who wishes to produce the best work that he is capable of producing ", affirms one critic categorically,[1] " must first of all become a socialist in his practical life, must go over to the progressive side of the class-conflict."

" The social organism to which literature has to be related ", asserts another critic,[2] " is humanity in its advance to socialism. The function of criticism is to judge literature, both content and form, as part of this movement. It can only fulfil this function if it takes part in the movement on the side of the workers of the world."

We notice that in both passages the emphasis falls on the class-conflict and this provides a clue to the whole Marxist ethos. For Marxists art is only important in as far as it helps or hinders the ' Struggle '. Whatever glorifies the ' Struggle ' is ' good ' and is encouraged, while whatever hinders it is ' bad ' and is mercilessly suppressed. The ' Struggle ' has been the most fruitful source of inspiration in Marxist art. The authentic poetry of the Russian Revolution is to be found not in Russian literature, but in Russian films. The work of Eisenstein and Pudovkin is important because it expresses a vital issue, because it shows *the people as a whole* united in a single movement. The great value of Eisenstein's work comes from the artist's concern for *life*, from the way in which he has caught the vitality and the energy that were released by the Revolution. From an artistic point of view it is the weakness of his films that the vitality remains somehow unattached, unrelated to any significant scheme of life.

Unfortunately, however, the new order has been somewhat slow in emerging and the sudden flagging of inspiration in the later Russian films shows that the source of inspiration was capricious. A revolution is of its nature sudden and short-lived. It may produce

[1] Edward Upward in *The Mind in Chains*, London, 1937, p. 52.
[2] Alick West, *Crisis and Criticism*, London, 1937, p. 140.

a series of masterpieces over a comparatively short period, but it must be followed either by a new order or by a fresh revolution. Art cannot thrive by presenting a permanent state of revolution. The decline of Marxist art in Russia has been accompanied significantly by an attempt to formulate a hard-and-fast theory of art and to impose it on all artists. Now the existence of literature depends upon the absolute freedom of the artist to express himself *through* existing society. The attempt to impose a rigid ' general line ' of thought on the artist is nothing more or less than an attempt to force the note, to make him portray a society which the ' Struggle ' has failed notoriously to bring into existence.

The Marxists' desire to bridge the divisions between the different sections of the community described above has led to the formation of two distinct and mutually hostile movements, each of which claims to be Marxist—Socialist Realism and Surrealism. Although Socialist Realism has been adopted by the Marx-Engels-Lenin Institute as the official Marxist theory of art and Surrealism anathematised as a Marxist heresy, both contain elements which are worth attention while remaining essentially one-sided and incomplete. They are both attempts to find a common basis for art, but they approach the problem from opposite angles. Socialist Realism is based on a materialist philosophy and Surrealism (in spite of an uncomfortable alliance with dialectical materialism) on an idealist philosophy. One seeks its common basis in the reality of the external world—in the thing perceived : the other in the unconscious life of the individual—in the perceiving subject. To the socialist realist individualism and introspection are anathema : the surrealist hopes by penetrating into the unconscious to reach a level which is beyond class distinctions.

Its insistence on the reality of the external world—the one fragment of truth salvaged from the wreckage of traditional philosophy—is probably the most important aspect of Socialist Realism and a corrective to the excessive subjectivism of some of the most distinguished of contemporary writers. It is also its most serious danger. For though Marxists deny any connection between Socialist Realism and Naturalism, it is clear that the conflict between Socialist Realism and Surrealism is the last phase of the struggle between Naturalism and Romanticism. Socialist Realism is nothing but Naturalism with the addition of a revolutionary ferment.

The danger of Socialist Realism as of Naturalism is the assumption that there is no other reality except the material reality of the world in which we move. The dogmatic application of this principle must lead, as it has led in Russia, to a complete impoverishment of art. Anything that does not fit in with the official view of life is brutally suppressed. This means that the whole development of modern literature is treated not merely as one-sided and incomplete, but as mistaken and its undoubted discoveries ruthlessly discarded. This poverty of outlook suggests that there must be something badly wrong with the programme of reconstruction in the name of which it has been elaborated. And in fact an incomplete conception of the meaning of terms such as ' class ' and ' social consciousness ', a failure to see that social and economic changes are themselves conditioned by something outside them, leads in practice to the assumption that our problems can all be solved by a simple economic and social reshuffle.

It is on these points that Surrealism, at any rate from a theoretical point of view, constitutes an important challenge to the assumptions underlying orthodox

F 2

Marxism. For the surrealist does appreciate that material reality is only one aspect of the real and his experiments justify the assertion that there are other aspects which, whatever one's inclination, cannot be disregarded or suppressed. Carried to its logical conclusion, Socialist Realism means a return to a more primitive mentality instead of a further development which would enable the discoveries of modern writers to be incorporated into a proper scheme and seen in their true perspective. Here again the surrealist has a contribution to make. For he sees that the ' new order' must be metaphysical and not merely economic, that it must begin instead of ending with a change in man himself. For what we need is first and foremost a spiritual revolution which will produce the social revolution. Although the surrealist is no more able to accomplish this than the orthodox Marxist, he is not prevented from demonstrating in a very forcible way its necessity.[1]

II

It is time to turn from general considerations to the Marxist poetry produced in this country. The more sensitive English Marxists have perceived the folly of attempting to impose a rigid theory on the artist and the attempt has been vigorously opposed by a writer like Mr. Stephen Spender in his book of criticism, *The Destructive Element*. It is evident from Mr. Spender's own verse, however, that there are other ways in which a particular philosophy may damage poetry. In one of his poems he writes :

> Leave your gardens, your singing feasts,
> Your dreams of suns circling before our sun,
> Of heaven after our world.

[1] This is discussed more fully in an article on ' Surrealism ' in *Arena*, for October, 1937.

Instead, watch images of flashing brass
That strike the outward sense, the polished will
Flag of our purpose which the wind engraves.
No spirit seek here rest. But this : No man
Shall hunger : Man shall spend equally.
Our goal which we compel : Man shall be man.

In Russia art inspired by the ' Struggle ' was some-
times a success, because the issue was a living one as
it has never been in England—as we can see from
these lines. There is clearly an attempt to work up
some sort of revolutionary fervour. The ' singing
feasts ' and the ' dreams of suns circling before our
sun ' are relics of romanticism and an appeal to a
shallow unbelief. The ' flashing brass ', the ' polished
will, Flag of our purpose ' are part of a sentimental
attempt to evoke the Marxist panacea. The high-
sounding words with their suggestions of hardness
and determination are, indeed, used to hide the obvious
immaturity which is so apparent in Marxist poetry ;
but they fail to cover the falsity of the emotion or
to enable the writer to carry off the bathos of

Man shall spend equally.
Our goal which we compel : Man shall be man.

Mr. Auden, on the other hand, provides a marked
contrast to Mr. Spender, with whom he is usually
bracketed. Auden has lately been described by an
orthodox Marxist as ' a bourgeois artist ' who has
entered into an ' anarchist alliance with Marxism '.
To the non-Marxist such criticism must appear as a
tribute to Mr. Auden's honesty and integrity. His
finest work is distinguished by a refusal to accept the
Marxist simplification. Its dramatic power springs
from an intense desire for social health combined with
a recognition of a state of necessary sickness. It is too
readily assumed that his poetry represents a ' healthier '
attitude than Mr. Eliot's, is in some way a ' fresh

start' in English poetry. It is his resemblances to
Mr. Eliot and not the differences between them that
are remarkable. The individualism and subjectivism
which are anathema to Marxists are not less, but more
pronounced in his work, as we can see from his fond-
ness for clinical associations and terms drawn from
Freudian psychology :

> Send us power and light, a sovereign touch
> Curing the intolerable neural itch,
> The exhaustion of weaning, the liar's quinsy,
> And the distortions of ingrown virginity.

The 'Struggle' dominates Auden's work as it
dominates that of his Marxist contemporaries, but it
is significant that he interprets it in a very different way
from them.

> You talk to your admirers every day
> By silted harbours, derelict works,
> In strangled orchards, and the silent comb
> Where dogs have worried or a bird was shot.
> Order the ill that they attack at once :
> Visit the ports and, interrupting
> The leisurely conversation in the bar
> Within a stone's throw of the sunlit water,
> Beckon your chosen out.   Summon
> Those handsome and diseased youngsters, those women
> Your solitary agents in the country parishes ;
> And mobilise the powerful forces latent
> In soils that make the farmer brutal
> In the infected sinus, and the eyes of stoats.
> Then, ready, start your rumour, soft
> But horrifying in its capacity to disgust
> Which, spreading magnified, shall come to be
> A polar peril, a prodigious alarm,
> Scattering the people, as torn-up paper
> Rags and utensils in a sudden gust,
> Seized with immeasurable neurotic dread.

This is a description of the ' Antagonist ' marshalling
his forces. Now there is a curious ambiguity about

the ' Antagonist ' who stands sometimes for what one writer calls ' the forces of inert habit within the decaying system ' [1] and sometimes, as he appears to in this remarkable passage, for the forces of revolution which will overthrow the doomed social order. The contrast between the obliviousness of the doomed society and the feverish activity of the agents is suggested by two sets of images—one suggesting stagnation (' silted harbour ', ' derelict works ') and the other suggesting force (' mobilise ', ' powerful', ' spreading magnified ', ' prodigious ', ' immeasurable '). The passage moves slowly at first and rapidly gathers momentum as it approaches the climax—the explosion of the subterranean force. There is a deliberate pause at

> Then, ready, start your rumour, soft

which creates a sensation of suspense which turns at once into fear. ' Horrifying ', ' disgust ', ' peril ', ' dread ' introduce the new motive—the fear of the victims which is heightened by the hiss of the s's. The last five lines rise to a roar. ' Spreading magnified ' makes the reader feel the hidden forces seizing the people, and is followed by

> A polar peril, a prodigious alarm

where the thud of the p's suggests the relentlessness of the movement carrying all before it. The whole is clinched by the final image of the rags, papers and utensils whirled by the wind.

It is curious that so sensitive a critic as Mr. Edgell Rickword should have been able to write of Auden that

" The setting-up of a pamphlet-poem antagonism, *i.e.*, social struggle *versus* inner struggle, is a reflection

---

[1] D. A. Traversi in *Arena*, October, 1937, p. 208.

of the poet's continuing isolation, falsifying the perspective of social development and delaying the re-integration of the poet into the body of society." [1]

For it is one of the most striking signs of Auden's integrity that he does realise that there is and must be an ' inner ' as well as ' social struggle ', and refuses to believe that the new order can be brought about by the simple economic reshuffle proposed by Marxists. The great problem that faces the modern poet is that he is without a ' system ' and that with all the good will in the world he cannot be re-integrated ' into the body of society ' as it is at present constituted, or adhere completely to any one of the conflicting groups, without entirely ruining his work. Auden therefore remains as much an isolated individualist as Mr. Eliot, and his best work simply registers a further stage in the social decay reflected in *The Waste Land*. The sense of the imminent collapse of the whole system has never been more vividly presented.

> Financier, leaving your little room
> Where the money is made but not spent,
> You'll need your typist and your boy no more ;
> The game is up for you and for the others
> Who thinking, pace in slippers on the lawns
> Of college Quad or Cathedral Close . . .

It is a striking fact that in Auden's poetry the emphasis falls almost exclusively on the destruction of the existing order and holds out no hope at all that a better order will emerge from its destruction. There never was a Marxist writer who was so completely uninterested in, so completely sceptical about the ' new order ' as Auden ; and this scepticism is evident from the flatness and emptiness of a poem like *The Dance of Death* which is supposed to show the emer-

[1] *New Verse* (Auden Double Number), November, 1937, p. 22.

gence of the 'new order' after the destruction of the old.

It is his honesty, his refusal to accept a facile solution which makes Auden's early work valuable as poetry and important as an indication of the plight of his generation.

CHAPTER VI

THE FUNCTION OF A CATHOLIC CRITIC [1]

" The touchstone is emotion, not reason. We judge a work of art by its effect on our sincere and vital emotion, nothing else. . . . A critic must be able to *feel* the impact of a work of art in all its complexity and force." (D. H. Lawrence.)

I

THE tendency of ' modern thought ' has been on the whole destructive, has been a continual process of dissociation. The rise of the positive sciences in the seventeenth century put an end to the old synthesis, or indeed to any kind of synthesis. Knowledge has broken up into the departmental sciences, which means that there has been an enormous increase in specialisation, in people who are equipped with a limited technique which is only capable of exploring one section of reality. The result has been twofold. Exponents of the departmental sciences have explored their corner of reality without making any attempt to relate it to first principles. The same men have tried to use methods suitable for one thing and one thing only to formulate a ' philosophy of life ' (Sir James Jeans, Freud).

In recent years people have become increasingly aware of the shortcomings of this method, and there has been a desperate effort, particularly among art critics, to put Humpty-Dumpty together again. The

[1] In order to make my position clear, I have been obliged in this chapter to quote extensively from other writers. These extracts are of the utmost importance for understanding the view I am putting forward, and should be read with special care.

necessity of some sort of synthesis seems to be inherent in the human mind. There is a desire for 'some system' which will provide the principles of art and also find a place for art in a general scheme of things. Thus in the middle of the nineteenth century we find Zola making comic efforts to found an æsthetic on Bernard's *Principles of Experimental Medicine;* and Brunetière (before his conversion) wrote a history of French literature based on a combination of Darwin and Haeckel !

In our own time the two most persistent attempts to provide a complete philosophy, and therefore to relate art and life, have been made by Catholicism and Marxism. We may not approve wholeheartedly either of Maritain's *Art and Scholasticism* or Trotsky's *Literature and Revolution;* but we must admit that both are healthy signs, because both are attempts to get away from doctrines like art for art's sake—one of the most chronic symptoms of the decay of bourgeois-capitalist civilisation. The advantage of a Catholic philosophy is that when properly applied it is capable of enriching the critic, of opening new horizons before him, while a materialist system necessarily impoverishes him and narrows his outlook on account of its exclusiveness. A Catholic philosophy provides the most comprehensive picture of the universe ; it is capable of finding a place for 'all experience', particularly for those experiences which materialism is driven to explain away, to discount as abnormal or illusory because they belong to regions whose existence is incompatible with materialism. Moreover, as I have already suggested, a Catholic philosophy with its emphasis on the nature of man, is in a better position than another to determine what experiences are good for man.

Thus *in theory* a Catholic critic should be able to

recognise valuable experience wherever he meets it and whatever the general outlook of the writer happens to be. Paradoxical though it may seem, the first thing a Catholic must realise is that in the literary order dogma must never be applied dogmatically. To assume that only certain forms of experience are valuable or that only those experiences are valuable which are completely Christian, is to condemn oneself to sterility at the outset. They may be the most valuable experiences, but they are by no means the only valuable experiences. If we are to be true to the ideal of comprehensiveness, we must be able to sympathise with the fresh experiences that are evolved in the course of civilisation. *In practice*, however, it is precisely on this point that both Catholic and Marxist critics are open to the gravest objections. As soon as absolute truths enter the literary order, the critic who is committed to a system exposes himself to two dangers. He tends to praise works which express, or seem to express, the dogmas of his system. Thus theory perverts sensibility. As an example, we have the Marxist critic's enthusiasm for Shelley on account of his alleged ' revolutionary ' outlook, and the admiration of Catholics for a poet like Francis Thompson. The other error is to condemn writers simply because their outlook is at variance with one's own system, as a Marxist writer like Mr. Philip Henderson [1] appears to condemn ' bourgeois ' novelists like Mrs. Woolf, Mr. Forster and Mr. L. H. Myers, and Catholics condemn D. H. Lawrence. While the spectacle of the converted Brunetière resolutely damning anything and everything modern is scarcely one on which we can look back with pleasure.

The function of criticism, as Eliot has pointed out,[2]

[1] *The Novel To-day*, London, 1936.
[2] *Selected Essays*, p. 24.

is " the elucidation of works of art and the correction of taste ". This is not a plea for a purely literary criticism—literary criticism in the sense of neat appreciation is something in which we can no longer believe —but it does stress an important point. Criticism is a matter of sensibility as well as of intelligence. The first business of the literary critic is to discover whether the poem is good or not, whether or not it provides the reader with a valuable experience. It is only later that he can go on to pass judgement on the state of mind behind the work. For if the art is bad, if it is a dead thing, then it can have no vital relation to the society from which it springs, and there can be no earthly good in discussing its symptomatic aspects. Only the great writer can be an important symptom because what is happening to him, what is revealed in him, is also happening to society. What we also have to recognise is that we are constantly meeting works of art which we know are good but which are still a sign of an unhealthy state of society. The best instance is of course Baudelaire, who was probably the greatest European poet of the last century. But healthy or not, the fact remains that great poetry, even when it is the expression of a crumbling civilisation, possesses in some measure the same kind of power—a regenerative power—that belongs to the great literature of the stablest periods.

The point I wish to stress is that the critic must approach works of art *as works of art*, not as sociological treatises. The clue is not the poet's beliefs or his morality, but his style. Francis Thompson and D. H. Lawrence have already been mentioned and they provide an excellent instance of what I mean. Francis Thompson's *Hound of Heaven* may, as a distinguished preacher once argued, be an excellent ' retreat book ', but the soundness of its theology or the ' majesty ' of its central idea does not concern the critic. What does concern him is that the language of the poem is tired, stale, effete. On the other hand, the justification of *Lady Chatterley's Lover* is that the ' lurid ' passages, so far from being unhealthy, are in fact written in a language which (as compared with Thompson's) is remarkably virile and fresh.

The danger with the dogmatic critic who is deficient in sensibility is that criticism will degenerate into a half-and-half science, will become a branch of sociology. This is the menace of a writer like Henri Massis who, whatever his qualifications as a thinker, is certainly deficient in sensibility.

" The dissolution of the human person ", he writes,[1] " is the feature that strikes us in the most recent manifestations of our young literary men, the disciples of Marcel Proust and André Gide, for example. . . . All the characters drawn by our young authors are recognisable by the fact that they are no longer *centred*, and this gives them a strange resemblance to each other that is well adapted to distinguish them from all the human types that have hitherto appeared in French literature. There is about them something loose, something like a refusal to be formed, and to make a unity of their discordances. There is no effort to concentrate on any point in their sensibility, but an entirely material sincerity in which the mind no longer plays a part. Not only have their intelligence and will no distinct aim, but it seems that the subject itself is looking for an undiscoverable ' ego ', as if modern subjectivism must finally result in a total dilution, a complete reabsorption into the original confusion of things. . . . It is the lassitude of a generation which was bruised too soon by life, and which has no discipline of heart or mind to defend it against a feeling of powerlessness to which many dis-

[1] *Defence of the West*, English translation, London, 1927, pp. 151-2.

appointments have made it prone. It is here that 'Asiaticism' lies in wait for us."

The interest of this passage lies in the fact that it is an illustration of the wrong use of the dogmatic principle. Massis bases his criticism on the Catholic view of man and has no difficulty in showing that the disciples of Proust destroy the unity and integrity of man and that their work is thoroughly subversive. But one cannot help feeling that criticism of this sort is not only too easy, but is also largely irrelevant. Instead of using philosophy to help literary criticism, Massis is actually condemning the writers on grounds which have nothing to do with literature and passes over the real virtues and the real vices of their work. For this is not literary criticism at all. It is simply using literature to try to prove the corrosive influence of Asiatic thought on European society. From a literary point of view, the cardinal defect of this school is its failure to get outside the narrow circle of purely personal feelings to something beyond, and of this Massis has nothing to say. Nor has he anything to say of its great merit, which is to have explored with unsurpassed insight whole new regions of human experience. Instead, we are fobbed off with a sentimental phrase about " a generation which was bruised too soon by life ". What we have to remember— what Massis seems not to remember—is that success of a work of art *qua* art is to a certain extent independent of the beliefs on which it reposes. It may still provide us with valuable experiences, even when it seems, in the Père de Munnynck's vivid phrase, to " propel humanity towards the abyss ".[1]

This does not mean that the psychological novel is not open to criticism. The way in which Catholic theology, properly applied, can facilitate the task of the

[1] *Colosseum*, March, 1934, p. 30.

critic, is brilliantly illustrated by Jacques Rivière's comparison between Stendhal and Dostoevsky.

" There is a sort of naiveté about every non-Christian writer. He always reminds you of someone from whom something is hidden without his suspecting it. . . . Even when it is no longer a question of penetrating into things, but simply of inventing people and happenings, even in the novel, Christianity gives a special power, a sort of extra profundity to anyone who seeks inspiration from it. Think of Stendhal, of the power and life he manages to give to his characters ! How briskly they move ! One perceives their feelings carefully grouped in them, always alive. The author rejoices in them as though they were delicious perfumes which would vanish the moment one breathed them in. They are all marvellously light, active, clear-cut. They are *individuals*—but not *creatures*. They are nothing but the sum of their passions. They are exactly what they feel and nothing beyond. In the last resort, their souls might have been composed by chemical forces sublimated to the *n*th degree (Stendhal believed in Cabanis). The one thing that is needed to make them absolutely real is this—one could never wish for them to be forgiven ; one could never pray for them. And just as we are separated from them, so they are separated from one another. . . . At bottom, they are without that little break which enables a human being to escape, to communicate with his neighbour. In them, humanity is without its wound. On the other hand, the characters of Dostoevsky have from their origin this other dimension. They are completely man, but also what man has from God. They begin by coming to life, and with what power and what zest ! They give way, without a thought, to the torrent of their individuality. They break down all resistance, they are as wicked as they can be. . . . And yet there is something more in them than their feelings. It is that faint image of God which never quite disappears. They can be saved. They have souls like us which may be lost. . . . There is more to it than that. They are not only so much alive that we fear for them ; but however base they may be, they have feelings which are unknown to the pure heroes of Stendhal." [1]

The reason why this criticism is illuminating is because it is *literary* criticism ; it shows that for Stendhal the absence of a coherent view of life involved artistic flaws in his work. It is instructive to compare the approach of Rivière with that of Massis in the passage given above. We notice at once that Rivière is concerned with the *writer*, and Massis with the *subject-matter* of the writer. Rivière shows how narrowness of vision leads Stendhal to present an incomplete picture of life, to exclude whole tracts of experience. Massis, on the contrary, is criticising the modern novel because its picture of man differs from man as defined in a Catholic philosophy, forgetting, it seems, that modern man has indeed lost his bearings and that the contemporary novelist's business is not to show us the ideal, but man as he is.

The great value of these two passages is the way that they bring out the difference between the literary critic and the sociologist. When we indulge in criticism of this sort we must be sure that we are criticising the artist and not the situation. " They are nothing but the sum of their passions "—it is a radical criticism of the modern *novelist*. No one will deny that the modern novelist's power of psychological analysis has enriched his art considerably ; but there has unhappily also been a corresponding loss. It was no doubt a mistake on the part of the older critics of fiction to insist on character to the exclusion of all else. But we are beginning to discover that character does matter.

[1] *De la foi*, Paris, 1927, pp. 72–4.

The character after all—the person who ' suffers ' the experience, to use a scholastic term—must be a *person* if his experience is to have any meaning for us. The genius of the modern novelist is to have presented with unprecedented power and vividness certain states of mind : his shortcoming is to have lost sight of the person in the state. The result is that the work of a writer like Mrs. Woolf is inclined to degenerate into a succession of intense but largely unrelated moments and nothing more. In other words, instead of the English novel developing and combining the characterisation of the old writers with the increased insight of the new, it has relinquished all that writers like Defoe, Fielding and Jane Austen had won.

II

The main point I wish to make is that dogma can only be used as a corrective. It cannot be applied in the narrow way in which a good many critics have tried to apply it. A good illustration of what I mean is provided by Rémy de Gourmont's devastating essay on Brunetière. He quotes a passage from Brunetière's book on Balzac :

" It is not only not true that everything appears differently to different people according to personal idiosyncrasies . . . but reality is the same for all intelligences. There is only one point of view from which it is true and ' in conformity with its object ', just as in science there is only one formula that is truly scientific."

Gourmont comments :

" With this principle one ends by denying the legitimacy of all individual activity. Art disappears altogether. . . . Every object, every fact, only permits of one valid representation, which is true, and ideas are necessarily divided into two classes—the true and the false. . . .

" Let us remain true to the principles of subjective idealism which are impregnable. The world is my representation of it. It is the only creative principle, the only one which allows the full development and ordering of intelligence and sensibility." [1]

There are two criticisms to be made of these passages. Brunetière, instead of using dogma as a corrective, tries to force one of the principles of moderate realism and ends by vitiating æsthetic judgement ; and Gourmont appears to seek in modern art the justification of a particular philosophical system. It is perfectly true that the development of modern art has been greatly influenced by the change from a classical metaphysic to idealism ; but this in itself tells us nothing about the *value* of the art nor about the truth or untruth of the philosophy. What we have to admit is that the works produced are often extremely good and that they have greatly increased the scope of our personal experience. What is more, the dogmatic application of Brunetière's principle would necessarily be sterile and deadening and would end in the most thorough-going academicism. We should be obliged to condemn the whole of Picasso's later work, superb as it often is, as well as nearly all modern poetry from Baudelaire and Laforgue down to Eliot, Pound and Auden.

On this particular issue the Catholic critic adopts an intermediate position. The real question is whether art ought or ought not to be representational. It is the old issue between Plato and Aristotle all over again. The tendency of modern criticism to minimise the importance of Aristotle's μιμησις strikes us as mis-

---

[1] *Promenades littéraires*, III., pp. 32–3.

taken. There is nothing to show that by ' imitation '
Aristotle meant a slavish ' copying ' of the object. He
was simply concerned to stress the representational
element—an element that always played a big part in
so-called classic art. The basic principle of represen-
tation—that there must be a relation between art and
concrete *things* and that the emotion must be propor-
tionate to the object that evoked it—seems to me to
be undeniably true. Whatever liberties the artist takes
with his material, there must subsist " the primitive
relation with the real " [1] if the work is to be intelli-
gible. For the conformity of emotion and object is
the only check to the cult of complete subjectivism
which has in recent years invaded all the arts.

I would suggest, parenthetically, that there is no
better way of estimating the value of Catholic philo-
sophy to the literary critic than by comparing the best
of Gourmont's criticism with the best of Rivière's. It
is an unfortunate fact that Rivière's output was small
and piecemeal, and some of his finest work is still
buried in the files of the *Nouvelle Revue Française*, where
it originally appeared. But it does show in what sense
Catholicism is a plus quantity, just as to my mind we
can now see that the scepticism of Gourmont, far from
being the brilliant intellectual advantage it was once
thought to be, was in fact a defect of intelligence that
prevented him from being a still greater force in
contemporary letters.

III

There is a final point that calls for comment and
explanation—the position of the Catholic critic in face
of contemporary literature. In an essay on ' Litera-
ture and Religion ' [2] T. S. Eliot draws attention to the

---

[1] *Colosseum*, September, 1934, p. 56.
[2] *In Essays Ancient and Modern.*

damage that is being done by the secularist literature of our time.

" Though we may read literature merely for pleasure, of ' entertainment ' or of ' æsthetic enjoyment ', this reading never affects simply a sort of special sense : it affects us as entire human beings ; it affects our moral and religious interests. And I say that while individual modern writers of eminence can be improving, contemporary literature as a whole tends to be degrading. . . . " [1]
" For the reader of contemporary literature is not, like the reader of the established great literature of all time, exposing himself to the influence of divers and contradictory personalities ; he is exposing himself to a mass movement of writers who, each of them, think that they have something individually to offer, but are really all working together in the same direction. And there never was a time, I believe, when the reading public was so large, or so helplessly exposed to the influence of its own time." [2]
" What I do wish to affirm ", he continues, " is that the whole of modern literature is corrupted by what I call Secularism, that it is simply unaware of, simply cannot understand the primacy of the supernatural over the natural life : of something which I assume to be our primary concern." [3]

It is clear that in such circumstances the critic finds himself in a sort of no-man's land—in territory which belongs at once to the theologian and the literary critic. There has been in the past, I believe, a tendency to confuse the two : we have had literary critics who have suddenly abandoned their rôles and turned theologian ; and we have also had the pronouncements of theologians like the late Abbé Bremond, who

[1] *Op. cit.*, pp. 105-6.
[2] *Ibid.*, pp. 107-8.
[3] *Ibid.*, p. 108.

were not sufficiently familiar with literary technique to venture into such realms at all. What I wish to do is to make Mr. Eliot's judgements an opportunity for commenting on the relation between the theologian and the critic, for indicating what seems to me to be the limitation of literary criticism as such.

I have taken it as axiomatic in this essay that ' pure appreciation ' is all over and done with, that the critic of literature must also be a critic of the culture from which that literature springs. His approach must be literary. He can show, for instance, how changes of style reflect changes of mind, how the disappearance of the classic virtues of objectivity and impersonality point to profound disturbances in the life of a people. He can also point out that *from a literary point of view* the disappearance of religious sanctions and the invasion of secularism has resulted in a tremendous impoverishment of poetry.

It seems evident, however, that the function of the literary critic, even the Catholic critic, once he enters this sphere, must in a sense be negative. He can show what has been lost, he can assert the need of Tradition and of a new social order ; he may even help to preserve Tradition where it exists ; but he can do nothing to get Tradition back for us once it has been lost, neither can he reform the existing social order. The weaknesses of the best contemporary poetry are inherent in society and they will only disappear when that society has given way to a better one. The literary critic can point all this out, he can diagnose, but with diagnosis his function as a critic comes to an end. The rest concerns his responsibility as a man.

" We shall certainly continue to read the best of its kind of what our time provides : " runs the concluding sentence of Eliot's essay, " but we must tirelessly criticise it according to our own principles and not merely according to the principles admitted by the writers and by critics who discuss it in the public press." [1]

" The recovery of religious sanctions in some form seems necessary to the health of the world ", writes another distinguished critic,[2] but, as he hastens to add, " they cannot be had for the wanting ".

It is abdication to be sure. But one can only commend the perspicacity and the humility with which two critics, writing from very different points of view, make the gesture of abdication.

[1] *Ibid.*, p. 112.
[2] F. R. Leavis, in *For Continuity*, London, 1933, p. 173.

BIBLIOGRAPHY

In addition to the books mentioned in the text, the reader is referred to the following works for a further discussion of some of the problems dealt with in the essay, and also as an indication of the way in which modern critics approach the literature of their own time.

ARNOLD, M. *Essays in Criticism*. (First Series.) MacMillan. 3*s*. 6*d*.
> [Essay on 'The Function of Criticism at the Present Time.']

LEAVIS, F. R. *New Bearings in English Poetry*. Chatto & Windus. 6*s*.
> [Probably the most satisfactory account of contemporary English poetry that has been written.]

MURRY, J. M. *The Problem of Style*. Oxford University Press. 6*s*. 6*d*.

READ, H. *Phases of English Poetry*. Hogarth Press. 3*s*. 6*d*.
> [Chapter on 'Poetry and Religion.']

THOMPSON, D. *Reading and Discrimination*. Chatto & Windus. 3*s*. 6*d*.

TURNELL, M. 'The Poetry of Jules Laforgue' in *Scrutiny* for September, 1936.
> [Influence of Laforgue on T. S. Eliot.]

WILLIAMSON, H. R. *The Poetry of T. S. Eliot*. Hodder & Stoughton. 5*s*. *Out of print*.
> [Introduction to T. S. Eliot for the plain reader.]

WILSON, E. *Axel's Castle*. Scribners. 10*s*. 6*d*.
> [First and last chapters contain a valuable account of the background of modern poetry. Excellent studies of James Joyce and Marcel Proust.]

WOOLF, V. *The Common Reader*. (First Series.) Hogarth Press. 5*s*.
> [One of the best volumes of critical essays written in our time. See particularly essays on 'Chaucer and the Pastons,' 'Modern Fiction' and 'How it Strikes a Contemporary.']

WOOLF, V. *Mr. Bennett and Mrs. Brown*. Hogarth Press. 2*s*. 6*d*.
> [An essay on the contemporary novel.]

TE L